W9-BQT-122

Manage
Projects

Manage Projects

Meet your deadlines and achieve your targets

ANDY BRUCE
KEN LANGDON

**LONDON, NEW YORK,
MUNICH, MELBOURNE, and DELHI**

Produced for Dorling Kindersley
by **terry jeavons**&**company**

Project Editor	Fiona Biggs
Project Art Editor	Terry Jeavons
Designer	J. C. Lanaway
Special Photography	Mike Hemsley
Senior Editor	Simon Tuite
Editor	Tom Broder
US Editor	Margaret Parrish
Senior Art Editor	Sara Robin
DTP Designer	Traci Salter
Production Controller	Stuart Masheter
Executive Managing Editor	Adèle Hayward
Managing Art Editor	Nick Harris
Art Director	Peter Luff
Publisher	Stephanie Jackson

First American Edition, 2007

Published in the United States by DK Publishing,
375 Hudson Street, New York, New York 10014

07 08 09 10 11 10 9 8 7 6 5 4 3 2 1

ED252—September 2007

Published in the United Kingdom by Dorling
Kindersley Ltd.

A catalog record for this book is available from
the Library of Congress

ISBN: 978-0-7566-3172-7

DK books are available at special discounts when
purchased in bulk for sales promotions, premiums,
fund-raising, or educational use. For details, contact:
DK Publishing Special Markets, 375 Hudson
Street, New York, New York 10014 or
SpecialSales@dk.com.

Printed and bound in China by Leo Paper Group
Discover more at www.dk.com

Contents

1 Create the Vision

2 Plan the Project

Introduction

Project management is no longer the preserve of the engineer. Today's organizations know that any series of activities aimed at a number of objectives should be considered a project and managed accordingly.

Whatever activity they are involved in, successful people recognize that the techniques and processes of project management will give better results more cost effectively.

Professional project managers recognize their individual projects in the context of the whole organization. They carefully go through the recognized stages of running a project, from creating the vision for the project to writing the

Best practice delivers results on time and within budget

important close-down report. They know that the plan's the thing that will achieve the project's objectives, involve all the key stakeholders, and gain commitment that the necessary resources will be available when they are needed and for the right amount of time. Whatever the size and complexity of the projects you are going to take on, you need to develop project management skills and use best practice processes to deliver results on time and within budget.

Manage Projects helps you to assess your current skills and then guides you through every aspect of the project management process. It shows you how to identify the activities involved in the project, prioritize them, and produce the network diagram that shows how they inter-relate. It helps you to focus on the critical activities, estimate the risks involved, and plan to avoid them or mitigate their consequences. Finally, it shows you how to monitor your progress, anticipate problems, and overcome any that occur.

If most of the activities you are involved in arise because of crises, this book will give you a step-by-step guide to getting the project under real control, and the activities involved planned well ahead. If the resources you need are never available at the time you booked them, or the resources are there but you are not ready for them because other activities have slipped, this book will show you how to correct this, achieve challenging project objectives, and receive the praise and admiration that you know you deserve.

Assessing Your Skills

The aim of this questionnaire is to get you to think about your skills in managing projects and assess your scope for improvement—so answer honestly. Complete it before reading the book, putting the appropriate letter in the "Before" box. After you have read the book and applied the techniques, complete the questionnaire a second time.

Before **After**

1 How do you distinguish project management from project planning?

A I don't see any difference between them.
B Project planning is about the detail of a project plan.
C Project management recognizes that a project can only add value in the context of other projects and the organization's aims; it includes the project plan.

2 Do you understand the value of projects to the organization?

A Sometimes they just have to be done.
B I have some idea of the costs and benefits.
C I prioritize the activities in the plan according to their value to the organization.

3 Do you set clear goals for projects?

A I am driven by the tasks I have to do.
B I have written down some objectives.
C I have a clear set of objectives and milestones that I have agreed with all the people with an interest in the project—the stakeholders.

4 Do you agree with the team about what, ideally, you want to achieve?

A I do not look at the ideal because it is unobtainable.
B I have a good idea of what is possible.
C I identify with the ideal of the team in order to get the best possible plan.

5 Do you understand the constraints you will have on resources?

A I am always constrained by time; everything is needed yesterday.
B I agree to resources as the requirement comes up.
C I look widely around the organization to see if there is any way that I can reduce the resources needed for projects.

6 How well do you estimate your resource requirements?

A I know roughly how many people I will need.
B I have agreed to the availability of the people I will need with their managers.
C I have high-level commitment to resources of people and all other resources such as equipment.

7 How effective is your network diagram?

A I'm not sure what a network diagram is.
B I have a list of activities and timeframes, but it's not documented as a network diagram.
C I use a network diagram to identify the critical path through the project so that I can focus on activities that could delay the project.

8 How well do you anticipate problems?

A I am too busy solving the current ones to think about future problems.
B I know where the major threats are and try to preempt them.
C I have thought through all the potential problem areas, taken action to avoid them, and created contingency plans should the threats occur.

9 Do you have in place a process for making critical decisions?

A I don't have time to go through a process and tend to go by my gut instinct.
B I will talk to members of the team before I make an important decision.
C I use a logical process involving appropriate team members and stakeholders and record how I arrived at the decision.

	Before	After

10 **How well do you think your communications plan works in practice?**

A I answer people's questions when they ask them.
B I keep team members up to date when we have our review meetings.
C I have a plan that makes sure that all stakeholders are given the information they need when they need it in an accessible form.

11 **How well do you lead the team through the different stages of becoming a team?**

A I don't know what the stages are.
B I just hope that eventually people will start to work together well.
C I recognize the four stages that all teams go through and help the team to become effective as soon as possible.

12 **Do you handle the cause of a problem rather than fix the effect?**

A I'm not sure what the question means.
B I find that quick fixes allow me to move the project along.
C Even when I have to put in place a quick fix because it is vital, I always look for the root cause and put that right.

13 **How useful are your progress reports?**

A Writing reports takes me away from getting on with the job in hand.
B I report to my sponsor on a monthly basis.
C I keep progress reports to the minimum, but make sure that everyone has the useful reports they need.

Final Scores

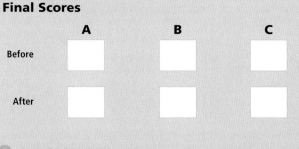

	A	B	C
Before			
After			

Analysis
Mostly As
Your answers suggest that you are fairly new to managing projects, and, while you may be enthusiastic, you need to think about the basic techniques of defining objectives and the planning process. Think first about your team's purpose and what it can achieve. Then work on the planning process to make sure you understand each stage and are confident how far you have got at any point in time. Think more about your stakeholders, particularly customers, and what they need and want.

Mostly Bs
You have some knowledge of managing projects and deal with your stakeholders and project team quite well. You are beginning to see your project from the organization's point of view but you need to put more time and energy into improving your skills in this area. Start with a team session and make a high level and methodical plan. Be very self-critical of your overall approach to project management.

Mostly Cs
You certainly have a professional approach to your role as a team leader and project manager. Make sure, however, that you establish a good rapport with your stakeholders and team members as well as treating them professionally. Concentrate on the long-term plan and use some of the techniques in this book to help to improve the environment in which you work and your results. Use these techniques to assist other people in your team to improve their skills. Show them how important it is to be in control of their work and their lives by reviewing and amending the project plan.

Conclusion
If this is the first time you have done this self-assessment, then bear in mind the analysis as you read the book. Pay special attention to the areas highlighted by your responses and take on board the tips and techniques—these will help you to reduce the number of A responses next time round and help you to achieve a more balanced mixture of Bs and Cs. After you have read the book and have had a chance to put the techniques into practice, do the quiz again. Provided you answer honestly, you will be able to measure your progress directly and should see a big improvement.

Create
the Vision

Successful projects can transform any
organization's effectiveness and efficiency.
Projects need effective project managers to
make sure that the benefits they will bring to
the organization happen on time and within
budget. This chapter will show you how to:

- Differentiate between project management
  and project planning
- Define a project and its stages
- Choose the projects that offer the most
  value to an organization
- Make sure that the project will improve the
  organization's environment as well as its
  operational performance
- Involve the stakeholders
- Check that the project is feasible

Today's Project Environment

People sometimes confuse project management with project planning. While good project planning is a vitally necessary part of project management, you will need to look at project management on a broader scale.

From Project Planning to Project Management

For many people their first exposure to any kind of project management is as a member of a project team that has a list of activities with time targets and designated owners. This activity list is part or all of a project plan. Historically, project planning was something that happened in industry, the domain of engineering departments, where detailed task and resource planning was required to complete complex engineering projects on time and within budget. Engineers developed a series of tools and techniques to manage large projects such as the building of a ship.

What Does a Project Manager Do?

Project management is more than simply completing a list of activities on time. Project managers also have to deal with issues that are critical to the success of the project, such as:

→ Motivating people.
→ Resolving critical issues.
→ Management of budgets.
→ Mitigation of risk.
→ The effective use of all of the organization's resources.

TIP **Brief your team members not only on their activities in the project but on their role in achieving the team and organizational goals.**

Adopt a Holistic Approach

Try not to get into the detail of a project plan too quickly. You can complete the plan but fail to meet the project's main objectives. Perhaps the customer no longer wants the product, the competition has launched a better one, or other internal resources have achieved the objectives of the project, thus rendering your plan irrelevant. Take a holistic view, starting from an understanding of what the customer needs, the requirements of the key stakeholders, and an awareness of how this project fits into the organization's overall project portfolio. Make sure that you align your project to one or more of the business goals of your organization and of your team. If a project does not help to deliver at least one key target, then either close it down or modify it to correct that fault.

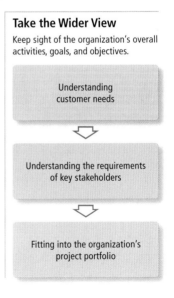

Take the Wider View
Keep sight of the organization's overall activities, goals, and objectives.

Understanding customer needs

⇩

Understanding the requirements of key stakeholders

⇩

Fitting into the organization's project portfolio

Define Projects

A project is a series of activities designed to achieve a specific objective within a specified period. You will improve your performance by identifying activities that will achieve their objectives on time and within budget.

Identify Projects

A project has clear starting and end points. It is driven by a number of objectives and a series of clearly defined activities taking the project manager from start to finish. Some projects are much more complex than others. It may be a straightforward task to paint the office, but that is just as much a project as is planning and building a bridge.

How to Use Project Management

Project management enables you to focus on priorities, track your performance, overcome difficulties, and adapt to changing situations. Tackling activities as projects allows you to use proven tools and techniques to lead your team effectively. It may take a bit of extra time in the early stages of a project to plan the activities and agree who is responsible for carrying them out, but in the long run tight project management will save time and increase the likelihood of a successful outcome.

think
SMART

The people with responsibility for activities within the project plan are key to its success, so it is important to keep them enthusiastic about the objectives of the project and about working with other team members.

Ensure that there is no culture of blame. It is difficult to work together if team members are defensive of their skills and will not listen to constructive criticism from each other. Encourage an environment where team members feel that they can make suggestions about how their colleagues could improve.

Identify the Key Features of a Project

Ask yourself if you would carry out your current activities more effectively if you treated them as a project. Look particularly at areas where your organization is trying to change the way it operates.

Establish whether you would work more effectively by treating activities as a project by asking:

→ Is there a defined starting and end point? Routine work can be distinguished from projects because it is recurring and there is no clear end to the process.

→ Would the activities benefit from a methodical approach? Good planning ensures that a project is completed on time and within budget, having delivered the expected results.

→ Do the activities need identifiable and separate resources? Projects are allocated resources of their own.

→ Is there a team of people involved? Projects usually need a team of people.

→ Can objectives be set? Projects usually have objectives to do with quality or performance.

Plan for Success If your project depends on the coordination of outside contractors, meticulous planning and organization will ensure that they are available to you when you need them.

Start Well and Carry Through Properly

It is important to start the project with a flourish and end on a positive note. Make sure that you understand the skills and techniques the team will need to be successful. The people who will be responsible for carrying out the activities detailed in the project plan are key to its success. Make sure that as well as the skills required they also have a strong interest in what the project is about and its success. The worst epitaph for any organization or project manager would be, "They never followed through." Yet many organizations start off a project with a big fanfare and then it slowly and quietly dies. Your job as a project manager is to make sure that the project is worth doing in the first place and then follow it through to completion unless a change in circumstances makes it irrelevant.

The First Stages in Project Development

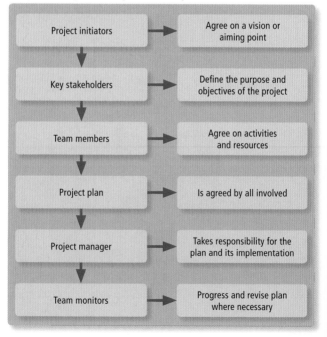

Project initiators	Agree on a vision or aiming point
Key stakeholders	Define the purpose and objectives of the project
Team members	Agree on activities and resources
Project plan	Is agreed by all involved
Project manager	Takes responsibility for the plan and its implementation
Team monitors	Progress and revise plan where necessary

> **No man that does not see visions will ever realize any high hope or undertake any high enterprise.**
>
> Woodrow Wilson

Create the Vision and Plan the Project

The first stage in a project is to show what it will achieve. Bring together all the core members of your team and any other stakeholders with an interest in the success of the project. List the project's measurable objectives, move on to action planning, and agree on the resources you will need. Order the project activities and schedule the tasks. Then validate the whole plan with everyone concerned to get their commitment to their part in the project activities.

Motivate the Stakeholders

The success of the project rests on your skill at selecting the right people, developing their skills, encouraging teamwork, and inspiring and motivating all the different personalities in your team. Ask your sponsor and other senior managers to demonstrate their commitment to what the team is going to do—start the project with as big of a splash as you can.

Implement and Monitor the Plan

Put in place an efficient monitoring system to plot your progress toward the objectives. The faster your monitoring system tells you about any slippages and problems the faster you can take action to resolve them. Ask for regular progress reports, organize team meetings, and identify milestones that will measure progress. When you have identified the potential problems and threats use logical processes to overcome them and alter the plan when required. Take notes so that you have a record.

Success rests on selecting the right people

Assess Project Priorities

You may find yourself with several projects to manage at the same time. Decide which projects are most important to your organization so that you can set priorities in allocating resources.

Prioritize by Value

Think about your organization's objectives as well as your own to assess which projects offer more value than others. A project that improves customer service, for example, may actually make a more valuable contribution than one that is mainly concerned with internal administration.

Plan Your Resources

Consider now how many resources each project requires. Your job is to deploy resources to those projects that will produce the greatest benefits for your organization. Discuss with your manager and the project coordinator the relative importance of each project before setting priorities. You may also need to discuss priorities with your customer or the key members of your team.

Case study: Prioritizing for Value

Jamila was a project manager for her organization's large paint shop. One of her projects was to clear an area and reequip it for powder coating warehouse shelving. She discussed priorities with Steve, her manager, who explained that although the sales strategy was to grow the warehouse shelving business, two very large orders for fencing had just been received, and this would delay the expansion into warehouse shelving. Jamila put her plans for clearing and reequipping the area on hold until the orders for fencing had been completed.

• By consulting over priorities, Jamila saw that the value to the organization of reequipping would not occur until later.
• Because she understood the real priorities she was able to allocate the resources for the shelving project into more valuable tasks.

Create a Master Schedule

Create a series of monthly columns on the right of the form. List all your ongoing projects, showing the time elapsed, and detail the resources you are likely to need to complete the projects.

	Jan	Feb	Mar	Apr	May	Jun	Jul	Aug
Project 1								
Project 2								
Project 3								
RESOURCES								
Project manager	1	1	2	2	3	2	2	1
Engineers	2	2	3	3	2	2	2	1
Installation staff	0	0	3	3	5	3	3	2
Specialized computer equipment	3	3	5	5	6	3	3	2
Low loader	0	1	1	1	2	0	0	1
Heavy crane	0	0	1	1	2	2	2	1

Produce a Project Schedule

To help you decide early on how to best handle a string of projects, create a master schedule. You may not be able to identify all the resources required at this stage, but you can make an estimate. This will enable you to see where there are potential resource clashes when more than one project requires the same resource. This in turn will drive the prioritization of projects. If, for example, two projects require a crane at the same time and there is only one available, you must reschedule one project. Using a master schedule takes time and may delay the start of projects, but it may also save time wasters during the implementation phase by avoiding conflicting resource requirements.

TIP Make sure that the priorities of the project and organization are aligned.

Define the Scope of the Project

The objective of a project is to assist a team in meeting its current operational objectives and to improve the environment for meeting increased targets. Make sure that you are taking a holistic approach to the project.

Use a Checklist

One of the best ways of establishing that all projects meet the criteria for success is to use a checklist so that you do not miss out anything when defining the scope of the project. A checklist ensures that:

- You are avoiding duplication and gaps in the overall project portfolio.
- Your project addresses real needs or exploits some opportunities that have been identified.
- Team members have a common understanding of how the project will contribute to the overall success of the organization and are committed to the project goals.

The checklist will be key to the success of the project and it is useful to start it as early as possible. One of the best checklists to use is SPRINT (Situation, Problem or opportunity, Risks of not doing the project, Impact, Needs, and Timing).

Involve the Team
If you are introducing a new system, involve the people concerned at all stages so that the implementation process will go smoothly.

Complete the SPRINT Checklist

Team members and key stakeholders will be much more committed to your project if you involve them in completing the SPRINT checklist. This will be key to the success of the project and it will be useful to start it as early as possible.

Gather together the key members of the project team to go through the SPRINT checklist in relation to your project:

→ **Situation**—Gather the information and facts that will drive the project's objectives and frame it in the context of team and organizational goals: "There is a drop in our retail sales and a strong growth in online buying."

→ **Problem or opportunity**—What problem is the team facing or what new opportunities could it exploit? "We could improve the effectiveness of our website in cross-selling second and third products rather than just selling the product the customer came online for."

→ **Risks of not doing the project**—"Our store managers may become demotivated when they realize where we expect to see sales growth."

→ **Impact**—What will be the quantified impact on bottom line performance? "We know that unenthusiastic stores sell 20 percent less per customer."

→ **Needs**—Based on the assessment of the issues the team faces, what are their needs? What is the purpose of this project? To improve the cross-selling of second and third products online.

→ **Timing**—What are the deadlines for achieving the agreed project objectives? "We are losing potential online business now; therefore the project is extremely urgent and should be completed within a year."

TIP **It may be impossible to complete SPRINT at the first try. Allocate fact gathering and other tasks to team members so that it can be completed later.**

Understand the Key Roles

Projects often involve people with very different backgrounds and skills. However, there are several pivotal roles necessary for the success of any project. Come to terms with the part each person will play.

Identify the Key Players

As project manager you take responsibility for the overall success of the project. Start off well by identifying the other key players and stakeholders and establishing good relations with them. The sponsor, often your manager, will be an important source of financial and moral support. The key team members will be responsible for parts of the project or groups of activities. Part-time or less senior team members may also make a contribution to the project plan and its implementation. Some projects may need experts and advisers with particular skills and knowledge. Stakeholders will include customers, suppliers, and people in different parts of the organization.

The success of a project depends on the key players

Involve the Stakeholders

Involve the stakeholders at the earliest possible stage in the project. Identify those who are key to your success and decide how often you will need to update them on the project's progress. Look for the stakeholders who are most enthusiastic about the project and enlist their strong support in motivating other people. Make sure you form good allegiances with those stakeholders who manage the resources of people, facilities, and money.

TIP **Obtain written agreements from resource managers showing when and in what quantity they will provide the promised resources to the project.**

The Key Roles in a Project

KEY PLAYER	ROLE
Sponsor Initiates the project	• Ensures that the project is relevant to the organization • Checks on the objectives and helps to identify constraints and risks • May provide resources
Project manager Responsible for achieving the objectives of the project and leading the project team	• Produces the detailed project plan • Motivates and develops the project team • Keeps stakeholders and other parties abreast of developments during the implementation of the project • Monitors key indicators to make sure the project is on track
Stakeholder Has an interest in the outcome of the project	• Gives valuable feedback to the project manager at different stages
Key team member Assists the project manager by bringing key skills and knowledge to bear	• Is a major contributor to the feasibility of the project plans • Has a direct responsibility for the project, delivering its promises on schedule and within budget • Often has necessary technical expertise
Team member Is engaged full or part time in carrying out project plan	• Takes responsibility for specific actions in the project plan • Sometimes fulfils a specialist role using expert skills and knowledge
Customer Benefits from the changes brought about by the project	• Has a lot of influence on the objectives of the project and how people will measure its success

Plan for Success

Essential ingredients for success in project management include defined and agreed upon goals, a committed team, and a viable and flexible plan of action. To achieve your goals, ensure that these essentials are in place.

Define Clear Goals

To be successful a project must have clearly defined goals. Agree to the goals with all the people involved so that everyone has the same goal. If they know what the objectives are they will be better able to respond to changes in circumstances that make some of their activities irrelevant; they will use the objectives as a guide to what to do instead. The scope of the project should remain consistent throughout. People who are significant to the project must commit their time to it and then stick to the commitment they have made. They are more likely to do this if they understand and are motivated by the benefits of achieving clear objectives.

Hope for the best, but be prepared for the worst

TECHNIQUES *to* practice

In project management it is important to set clear measurable objectives. You can practice this in many other areas of your life, for example when planning a vacation with your family. Get your family together to plan the break and identify their objectives for the vacation.

- Ask the individual members of the family to list their particular objectives.
- Negotiate a set of objectives that everyone agrees on.
- After the vacation establish whether or not the family's objectives were achieved by comparing them against the vacation experience.

Be Flexible

In a rapidly changing environment the ability to think ahead and anticipate can make the difference between achieving project objectives or not. Be prepared to change your plan by:

→ Re-evaluating the plan regularly.
→ Talking to individual members of the team and probing for changes in circumstances.
→ Anticipating the need for change as early as possible. Never continue with activities that you know should change.

It is unlikely that your original plan will be the one that you carry out all the way to the conclusion. Keep all your stakeholders up to date with your changing plans by putting in place good and regular lines of communication.

Choose a Team
As project manager, it is your responsibility to develop the best team possible, keep it on track, and ensure that the team members benefit from the experience and come out of the project with new skills. Choose your team carefully and provide training where necessary.

Gain Commitment to Your Plan
If your project is to succeed you will need other managers to commit to it. When you have developed your project plan identifying the people, facilities, equipment, and materials you will need, and when you will need them, make sure that everyone involved has seen it and agreed that the resources you require will be there when needed.

A man who enjoys responsibility usually gets it. A man who merely likes exercising authority usually loses it.
Malcolm Forbes

Check that the Plan is Feasible

Before starting the project, you need to be certain that there is a reasonable chance of achieving success. Ask questions to assess whether the project is properly timed, feasible, and worthwhile before going ahead.

Is the Timing Right?

However desirable a project may seem, check that it is the right time to carry it out. Without careful examination of timing you run the risk of failure, for a number of reasons:

- Other projects that are already started may make the project irrelevant. If, for example, a team is working on a complete revision of your organization's website, it may be better to delay the implementation of a system for buying online until the revision is complete.
- Your organization may be trying to implement too many projects at once. Those working on projects may also be responsible for achieving operational targets, and their involvement in the project may jeopardize these targets.
- Where projects are competing for the same, possibly scarce, resources it is vital that the right projects are done at the right time.

Postpone a project if there is a possibility that it won't produce a valuable result.

Assess the Situation You will need to ascertain whether it is really the right time to implement your project.

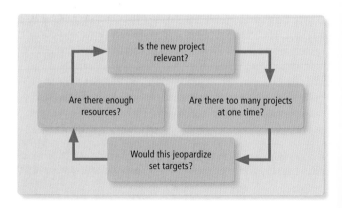

Is the new project relevant?

Are there too many projects at one time?

Would this jeopardize set targets?

Are there enough resources?

HIGH IMPACT
- Involving at an early stage those people whose jobs will change
- Doing a project at the right time for the organization rather than at the right time for your team

NEGATIVE IMPACT
- Presenting people with an instruction to change when the project is finished
- Moving on regardless when a project has lost relevance

Identify the Driving and Restraining Forces

Every project is driven by the needs of the organization. The stronger these needs, the "driving forces," the more likely the organization is to put energy and resources into the project to make sure that it succeeds. The reasons why particular projects are less likely to succeed, the "restraining forces," should be identified early on so that you can overcome them or change the timing of the project.

- The need to win back your customers from your main competitor is a driving force. A project that goals to do that will probably succeed as it will be clear to the organization how valuable the result of a successful project could be.
- The people involved in implementation may be concerned about changing how they carry out their tasks in order to implement the project. Where this resistance is strong it is a key resisting force, and will threaten the successful outcome of the project.

5 minute FIX

You can often come under pressure between the time that you complete the plan and start its implementation.

- Use a shortcut to check feasibility by highlighting potential problem areas.
- Make a list of the critical success factors for the project.
- Mark each one red, yellow, or green.
- A preponderance of yellow and green indicates that the project is feasible.

Predict Success

Making an accurate assessment of a project's feasibility involves knowing how the current situation in your organization will affect it for good or bad. Understanding what these different forces are allows you to predict how likely you are to succeed in achieving the objectives of your project. Forcefield analysis is a useful technique to help you to decide whether the project's driving forces outweigh the restraining forces and whether the overall balance is weighted toward success or failure.

Use Forcefield Analysis

To assess the relative impact of each force, use a scale of 1–5, where 1 represents a weak driver and 5 an essential organizational need. A restraining force that is not much of a threat to the project is represented by −1, while −5 indicates a force that is very strong and therefore puts the project at risk. Unless you can minimize the impact of this force it will probably be an obstacle to the achievement of the desired project results. Show your forcefield analysis to key team members and ask them to give you their opinion on whether you have correctly illustrated the forces that will have an impact on the ultimate success of the project.

Weigh the Balance Sometimes it's easier to weigh the options if they are presented graphically. This diagram illustrates the likely success or failure of a project very clearly.

Forcefield Analysis

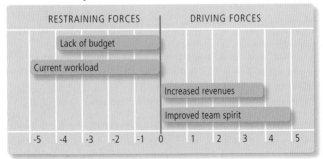

Types of Financial Benefit

List the financial benefits of the project to the organization under four headings to assess which are the most compelling.

TYPE OF BENEFIT	IMPACT
Reduction in costs	A cost that the organization used to incur will be eliminated by the project
Avoidance of costs	A cost that does not exist at the moment will be incurred later if the project is not undertaken now
Increased sales	The project will result in an improvement in revenues, internal or external
Improvement in management control	Managers will have better information on which to base decisions

The most compelling financial benefits that a project is most likely to realize are cost reduction and cost avoidance. The financial reasons for doing a project that will be seen as less likely to occur are an increase in sales and an improvement in management control.

Assess Financial Feasibility

A key factor in deciding on the feasibility of a project is the cost-benefit analysis that accompanies the project plan. Make a list of all the costs you will incur, then estimate what will be the financial benefits of the project to the organization. Estimating the benefits is the more difficult part of this exercise. For each of the benefits take advice from people with experience in the area or look at other parts of the organization where there has been a similar initiative. In the end, you may have to use three estimates:

- Pessimistic outcome
- Most likely outcome
- Optimistic outcome.

If the most likely outcome of the project is a financial benefit that outweighs the costs substantially, then it is very likely that the project will be financially feasible.

Summary: Creating the Vision

All projects are set up and driven by someone with a vision of what needs to be done. Think about the scope of your project and what the priorities will be. Get the right people involved and define their roles carefully. Check that the benefits to the organization are greater than the costs, and that your vision is stretching but feasible.

Planning for Success

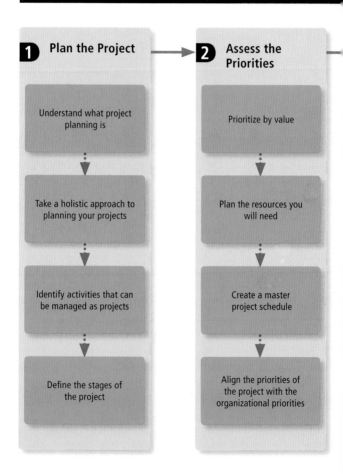

1 Plan the Project

Understand what project planning is

Take a holistic approach to planning your projects

Identify activities that can be managed as projects

Define the stages of the project

2 Assess the Priorities

Prioritize by value

Plan the resources you will need

Create a master project schedule

Align the priorities of the project with the organizational priorities

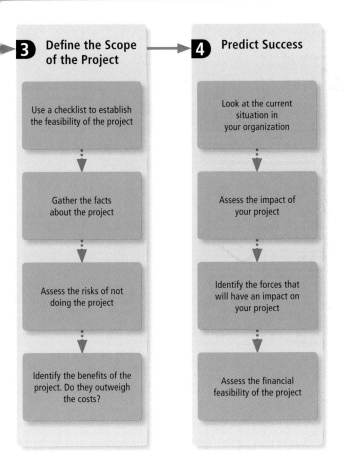

3 **Define the Scope of the Project** → **4** **Predict Success**

Define the Scope of the Project	Predict Success
Use a checklist to establish the feasibility of the project	Look at the current situation in your organization
Gather the facts about the project	Assess the impact of your project
Assess the risks of not doing the project	Identify the forces that will have an impact on your project
Identify the benefits of the project. Do they outweigh the costs?	Assess the financial feasibility of the project

Plan the 2 Project

Success in project management starts with success in producing a detailed project plan. To help you through the steps involved in creating a good plan, this chapter will show you how you can:

- Define a vision for the project
- Define clear and measurable objectives
- List and put in order the activities necessary to achieve the objectives
- Gain commitment to the resources you will need to complete the project
- Assess your skills as a leader

State Your Overall Goal

It is vital to understand what you want your project to achieve. Get together with your key team members and your sponsor to produce an overall vision statement toward which everyone can strive.

Define the Change You Want to Make

The goals of the project should be summarized so that everyone involved knows what it is expected to achieve. Create a statement that describes the project's vision. For the statement to explain your proposal properly it must ask, "What are we going to change and how?" Show the statement to your customers, who may refine it by describing what they would expect from it. If the project goals include something of real value to your customers that will be a good indicator of its desirability: a revamping of your sales order processing system might include an objective to reduce the amount of time customers spend correcting invoicing errors. Express this element of value to the customer in the vision statement. Meet with the key members of the team to outline the changes you wish to make. Tell them how achievable you think these changes will be. The statement should be stretching, but realistic, if people are to believe in the project.

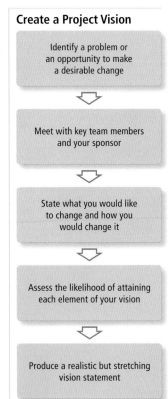

Create a Project Vision

Identify a problem or an opportunity to make a desirable change

⇩

Meet with key team members and your sponsor

⇩

State what you would like to change and how you would change it

⇩

Assess the likelihood of attaining each element of your vision

⇩

Produce a realistic but stretching vision statement

Strive to Achieve the Ideal

You are much more likely to get the vision statement right if you try to define the ideal outcome of the project. Real innovation takes place when someone decides that things could be different and much better. Ask your team members to describe what the project should change in an ideal world. Tell them that although they should remain rooted in reality, they should still think creatively. Do not allow the fact that you have been doing things in the same way for a long time to deter you from coming up with alternatives. Be careful when dealing with customers at this time. Explain that what you are describing is not how the world will definitely be, but how you would like it to be. Determine how feasible it is to attain your ideal. If you set yourself stretching objectives at the outset the project will deliver as much value as possible.

5 minute FIX

If your team is short of time to define the ideal identify an easily pleased and a difficult customer.

- Make one telephone call to each customer to get their version of the ideal.

- Let the team read and assess the responses of each customer and use this information to make adjustments to the plan.

Achieve Your Vision

HIGH IMPACT

- Allowing for compromise with the ideal in order to arrive at a feasible vision
- A clear and unambiguous statement that everyone can understand and strive toward
- Involving your customers so that they can make a contribution

NEGATIVE IMPACT

- Ignoring major obstacles in setting the vision
- Some key team members being sceptical about the feasibility of the vision
- Involving too many people so that you are required to make too many compromises

Set Your Objectives

Measure the progress and ultimate success of a project by defining a set of clear objectives at the start. Clarify your purpose, list the objectives, and then set priorities.

Be SMART

Expand the vision statement so that it explains what you are going to achieve, how long it will take, and how much it will cost. Now ask yourself which of these three is the most important driver—this information will provide a clear focus for the team. For example:

- **Time**—The outcome is very urgent.
- **Cost**—You must not exceed the previous year's budget.
- **Performance**—You need to neutralize a possible threat from the competition.

Now you are in a position to set the project objectives. To serve its purpose an objective must be SMART:

- **Stretching**—An objective has to be worth all the time, money, and trouble that will be spent on it.
- **Measurable**—You must be able to focus on a target and demonstrate at the end that you have hit it.
- **Achievable**—It has to be an achievable objective.
- **Relevant**—The objective will have no value if your customer does not benefit.
- **Time-targeted**—Everyone must know the due date.

Meeting Urgent Time Targets

Some projects require a very quick start. A health and safety issue at work, for example, may require a short project that will start immediately. Take steps to save the team time by:

→ Setting the objectives at a meeting with no junior team members present.
→ Limiting the objective to solving the immediate safety problem.

Keep a Record

Use a table to keep a clear record of the project's objectives, measures, priorities, current performance, and targets.

OBJECTIVE	PRIORITY	MEASURE	CURRENT	TARGET
Increase online sales orders	10/10	Revenues	$20 million	$40 million
Decrease delivery time	7/10	Average days from order to delivery	7 days	3 days

Prioritize Your Objectives

Rate the priority of each objective on a scale of 1–10, where 1 is the least important. It is usually easy to determine which objectives are very significant and which are not, but the ones in between may be more difficult to prioritize. Focus on the value that the objective offers to the business, taking into account one-time as well as ongoing financial benefits. Now set your target. This may be simply to increase sales by 25 percent, or it may be more difficult to specify.

A clear vision will produce a successful outcome

Set Your Target

If your objective is to improve customer satisfaction, then you will have to select a measure of satisfaction. If, for example, your goal is to reduce the number of customer complaints you receive, you will need to put in place a system to record the number of complaints that were made in a given period before you set your target.

TIP Think about how relevant the objective will be at the time the project is completed, and be prepared to drop any objective that has a low priority.

Assess Constraints

Every project has constraints. These may include time, money, or the availability of resources. Identify the constraints at the outset and ensure that each member of the team is prepared to work within them.

Don't Make Change for the Sake of Change

If something is working, it may be better to continue using it. Even if you identify an area that could be improved, it may be better to leave it to a later project. It is particularly important not to change your financial targets halfway through a project as part of a general improvement.

Make Change Gradually

If you change a lot of things at the same time it can become difficult to measure the outcome against the target because you cannot be sure which change produced which result. If you are running a business that has a very low profit margin, making too many changes at the same time could worsen your position and you may not realize which change activity has actually caused the decline.

Case study: Managing a Time Constraint

Larry was the project manager for a satellite television company that made available live television broadcasts to people flying in the customer's airplanes. The main constraint on the project was a tight budget.

When Larry realized that the Olympica were taking place approximately six months before the planned delivery date, he approached the customer and explained that they could deliver

in time for the Olympics if a bigger budget was available. The customer saw the opportunity and agreed to increase the budget.

• *By seeing that there was value to the customer in a faster project time frame Larry increased the value of the order, and overcame the problem with the budget.*
• *He improved his organization's reputation for creativity with a major customer.*

Look at Time Constraints

Frequently, a fast-moving business environment gives projects a specific window of opportunity. If a competitor is going to deliver a new line into stores for the summer season, you will have to work within that time constraint. There will be no benefit from working to deliver a competitive product if you cannot launch it in time. Don't accept an artificial constraint. If you can produce more value by adding three months to your deadline, make a case for having that constraint removed.

Seasonal Styles Industries such as fashion retail are often driven by time constraints—in this case the importance of getting a new line into the stores in time for the start of the new season.

5 minute FIX

If you are under a time constraint, decide what you are not going to include in the project.

- Make a list of side issues that you are going to ignore.

- Send the list to stakeholders for their agreement.

- Tell the team that the decision about which issues to ignore has been made and that no more time should be spent on them.

Understand Resource Constraints

All organizations work with limited resources and budgets, and they have to pass on these constraints to their project managers. A big, complex project may require a huge number of resources, so find out early on if these will be available, and at the right time. If your project depends on a level of resources that is unlikely to be forthcoming, change the objectives. If your organization is very intent on the achievement of the project's objectives you may encounter a lot of pressure to agree to try to achieve the current objectives with fewer resources than the minimum you think will be necessary.

- Hold your ground and prove your case to avoid getting into a situation where the project will fail.
- Volunteer a tight time frame if that will improve the outcome for the organization.

Double-Check Your Resource Requirements

Project managers tend to push for the maximum amount of resource that they can get to make sure that they can complete their projects on time with the best possible result. If they use more resources than they actually needed to complete the project the financial benefits of the project are reduced. Double check that you really need a resource by:

→ Making sure that each resource is "mandatory" to the project—that it will be impossible to complete the task without having access to that resource.
→ Looking at the non-mandatory resources with a view to finding an alternative way of completing their tasks or managing without them.
→ Asking people to be held on standby rather than joining the team; they can be brought on board when it becomes obvious that their role has become mandatory.

Use Existing Resources or Solutions

Look hard at the current situation. Other departments in your organization may have plans for change in an associated area so, in order to reduce the duration and cost of your project, you could capitalize on the plans and work of others. Perhaps you could use a shared component in your product design rather than engineering a new one, thus reducing design and production costs. It is important to reuse as much as possible. If, for example, the project includes a new business process, see if any other process software could be adapted to your situation. It is rarely a good idea to start from scratch, even if sharing in other people's work means making compromises. Once again it comes down to the cost of the project against the benefits it will produce. Using an already designed website, for example, may improve the cost/benefit analysis.

TIP **Limit the size of your team. People will be impressed with the outcome of the project, not with the number of people you have on your team.**

Draw up an Activity List

Now that you are aware of your objectives and your constraints, you are in a position to get into the detail of the activities required to complete the project. List all the activities and divide them into groups.

The Purpose of the Activity List

Breaking the project down into smaller work units or activities makes it much easier to identify overlaps, and to assess how some activities may affect the timing or the outcome of others—their inter-dependencies. It is likely to be a long list and it will help to divide it into groups or phases so that each set of tasks becomes more manageable and easier to track when monitoring performance and progress. Grouping also helps you to determine how activities fit into a logical sequence for completion. If an activity does not easily fit into a group, establish whether it is really necessary. Identify what should be delivered by the end of each phase as checkpoints on the way to achieving the overall project goals. This helps with scheduling and assessing the number of people and the skills that you will need. Listing activities in this way also reduces the risk of misunderstandings, since all the team members know what their tasks are.

Plan Project Activities

Brainstorm a comprehensive list

Group activities into a logical order

Check that nothing has been missed or duplicated

Give each group and activity a unique identifying number

Document the activity list clearly

Consult the Right People

Start the detailed planning process by drawing up a list of activities. Involve the appropriate people in creating the list. Try not to judge their contributions at this stage.

Involve the Right People You may need to involve stakeholders whose views will be valuable, people who are not full-time team members, and people who may join the project at a later stage.

Get Backing Consultation at this stage will tap into the expertise and experience of others, and will ensure that they will be commited to the implementation phase of the project.

Ask for Information You need to produce as comprehensive an activity list as possible, so keep checking to see if anything is missing. Ask for a concise, one-sentence description of each activity.

Schedule the Activities

Scheduling is another useful aid when grouping activities. Think about the logical order in which the activities will have to happen. One group may not be able to start before another group has been completed. Perhaps some activities are to do with an event later on in the project. When you arrange the activities in order you will be able to see the logical progression of the groups as they occur from the start to the finish of the project.

Look Out for Typical Groups and Gaps

Every project has three groups of activities in common, which together form a good starting point for the grouping exercise. The groups are:

- **Start-up**—Activities that signify the launching of the project, introduce team members, and record what each person has committed to achieving
- **Close-down**—Activities that check that the target performance indicators have been achieved and finalize the project documentation so that subsequent project teams and managers can benefit from your experience
- **Communications**—Activities that ensure regular communication between the project's stakeholders, such as issuing weekly progress reports or bulletins, or holding a familiarization presentation when a pilot program is about to begin.

When you have finished listing these groups and the others in the project go through the planned activities step by step to see if there is anything missing. Ask yourself if the completion of all of these activities will achieve the project objectives. It is important not to omit any activities since this could have time and budget considerations later on in the project. Once you are confident that each group of activities is complete, give each group and activity within it a unique identifying number.

TIP Make sure your activity list reflects the priorities that you set for the objectives.

Pre-empt Problems

GROUP	ACTIVITY
1	**CONDUCT ANALYSIS** 1.1 Interview customer focus group 1.2 Write report on findings 1.3 Present report to board
2	**AGREE PRODUCT OUTLINE** 2.1 Consult with all departments 2.2 Agree outline budget
3	**COMPLETE DESIGN** 3.1 Take first draft to representative customers 3.2 Amend according to feedback 3.3 Gain board agreement to design
4	**ARRANGE LOGISTICS** 4.1 Order materials 4.2 Train people 4.3 Select sub-contractors

Plan Progress An activity and group document will show, in detail, the progress of a product from inception to the beginning of the manufacturing process.

Pilot Your Project

One activity that many projects have in common is the setting up of a small-scale pilot program. This is an excellent way of assessing the likely benefits and drawbacks of implementing a new and complex project. Typical activities involved in piloting include:

- Inviting people to join a pilot team
- Implementing each phase of the project on a limited and controled basis
- Documenting the experience as you subsequently roll out the project to all the stakeholders.

Incorporating a pilot phase means that you will probably have a far less stressful and error-prone experience when you roll out the whole project. Choose the people for the pilot carefully, warning them that they are the first users and should expect some problems in the beginning.

Plan Resources

A full study of the resources you will need to implement the project is vital. Its feasibility depends on comparing an accurate estimate of the resources required with the benefits it will bring to the organization.

Estimate People Costs

The major cost of implementing a project is often the cost of the people involved. Think about who you will need for each activity and for how long you will need them. The project will have to bear the entire cost of the full-time members of the team. The cost of part-time members can be worked out by establishing the length of time they will spend working on the project.

Identify Other Essential Resources

There are resources apart from people that will have an impact on your budget. Look carefully at all the other resources you will need, for example market research, facilities, equipment, and materials. Examine the details of your requirements. If you will need to reserve a training room, it is not enough simply to know that you will need a training room for a period of a month during the project. You need to assess how large the room needs to be, the

TECHNIQUES
to practice

The ability to estimate resources and to calculate accurate budgets is vital in project management.
Practice your skills on a DIY project at home.

- Plan the detail of the project down to the number of screws you will need.

- Keep an eye on your budget as you do the project.
- Write down your actual expenditure against each item in your budget to see how accurate a budget you were able to prepare.
- If you went over budget, what did you fail to anticipate?

Discuss Your Needs At the early planning stages of your project discuss your resource requirements with suppliers.

equipment you will need, who will supply any necessary catering, and what the costs will be. Do not avoid the detail of your requirements. Knowing the detail ensures that you get the cost right and avoid a small error in each resource requirement causing a large error overall. The more detail you have at this stage the more likely you are to avoid problems during implementation. Making good estimates of resources now will enable your team to focus on achieving the project's objectives rather than on fixing problems caused by bad planning.

Think about Key Resources

How many people will you need?

⬇

What types of skills will they require?

⬇

Do you need facilities or materials?

⬇

Is more information or technology needed?

⬇

What is the total cost of the project?

⬇

Are sufficient funds available?

Make Effective Use of External Resources

While many resources will come from within the team or organization, you will probably need to go outside for others. External contractors can offer a cost-effective and efficient resource to a project.

Contractors may have skills and experience that your organization lacks and needs only temporarily. Form a good relationship with your contractors so that they feel that they are part of the team and committed to the objectives of the project.

→ Obtain competitive quotes from more than one potential supplier. Set a goal for three, since more than that will take a lot of time to evaluate and may prevent potential suppliers putting in the necessary effort to win the business.

→ Reach an agreement on performance that is easy for both parties to monitor. There should be an overall goal, an effective measure of their success, and agreement on when they should reach certain milestones.

→ Fix the list of costs against what the contractor expects to deliver. Make contingency for the additional things that will inevitably crop up.

→ Negotiate the best deal by making it clear that you have other options. Get help if you're an inexperienced negotiator and the deal is a complex one.

Do not be afraid of getting into very detailed discussions with a contractor. The tighter the agreement, the less likely it is that there will be conflict during the project. For complex projects you and your contractor may want to create a list of risks, how they will be managed, and who they will be managed by.

> **Of all the things I've done, the most vital is coordinating the talents of those who work for us, and pointing them toward a certain goal.**
>
> Walt Disney

Make the Most of Scarce Resources

Your organization will always look for the best return from the deployment of its resources. Be prepared to compromise on the resources you need for your project. Look for compromises that do not threaten your objectives. For example, you may be able to use someone less qualified if she is supervised by a key team member.

Create a Resource Matrix

The end product of resource planning is a document showing when you will need all the resources. This document is the basis for the commitment of all the stakeholders to supplying the necessary resources. Write this down in a matrix showing all the activities, the resources involved, who is responsible for what, and the cost. No organization or stakeholder can guarantee that events will not interfere with their commitments; but you are much more likely to obtain and retain resources if you can reach this agreement before starting the project.

Plan the Project Resources

Project: ABACUS CAMPAIGN

People	Who responsible	Who involved	Training needs
	Marketing manager	Marketing team	Interviewing skills
Time	2 days	5 days	1 day
Cost	$1,000	$10,000	$3,000
Resources	Facilities	Equipment	Materials
	Meeting room for 40 people	OHP, Chart, Computer	Market research questionnaires
Time	1 day	1 day	
Cost	$2,000	$500	$500

TOTAL COSTS $17,000

Get Agreement on Costs When you have identified all the resources you will need for a project, and have estimated your costs in detail, document these and seek your stakeholders' agreement to every element before proceeding.

Order the Project Activities

Not all activities will have to start at the same time in order to meet the project's planned completion date. Put activities into a logical sequence, estimate the duration of each, and then devise a project schedule.

Estimate Timings

An accurate estimate of the time each activity will take is crucial to creating an effective schedule. If you do not know how long it will take to do something, look for guidance from people, inside or outside the organization, whose experience will help you. Getting it wrong at this stage can throw the project off course. Make sure that the team members are involved in this estimation, particularly if they have previous experience, and get their agreement to the timing of each of their activities. If there is any doubt about how long an activity will take, estimate the worst and best case scenarios and use a compromise between the two.

> **Time spent on planning is never time wasted**

Create a Network Diagram

A network diagram shows the relationship between activities and which ones depend on the completion of others. The diagram will be simple or complex, depending on how many activities there are and how they interrelate.

Estimate the Total Time

Where there are several routes through a network, you can complete tasks simultaneously as long as they do not require the same resources at the same time. Use the time estimates you have made to estimate the total time it will take to complete each route and find the longest route. This longest route is known as the critical path and shows the shortest possible duration for the project.

Critical Path Analysis

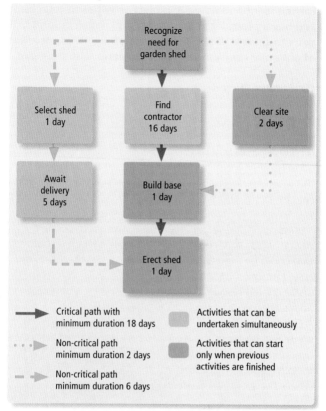

Recognize
need for
garden shed

Select shed
1 day

Find
contractor
16 days

Clear site
2 days

Await
delivery
5 days

Build base
1 day

Erect shed
1 day

→ Critical path with
minimum duration 18 days

⋯⋯▸ Non-critical path
minimum duration 2 days

– – ▸ Non-critical path
minimum duration 6 days

Activities that can be
undertaken simultaneously

Activities that can start
only when previous
activities are finished

Use Critical Path Analysis

**Create a Critical Path
Analysis** Show which tasks
are critical to the successful
achievement of the project.

Some activities will be critical to
completing the project on time; if
they slip by a week then the whole
project will slip by a week. Project planners use critical
analysis to identify the activities on the critical path.

- They put a lot of effort into making sure that these
  activities have no time slippage.
- They recognize that, as the project continues, time
  targets may be missed and the critical path may change.

Make a Schedule

Having identified how the project activities fit together, and having calculated the project's minimum duration, you can set real dates. Schedule carefully, taking account of potential conflicts, and agree to dates with the team.

Calculate Dates

Use the network diagram to calculate start and end dates for each activity, beginning with the first activity. Start each activity as early as possible to make as much allowance for slippages as you can. You can be more flexible with activities that are not on the critical path since they do not affect the overall duration of the project. Refer to your activity matrix and master schedule to check that the dates you have set are realistic. Finally, plot the dates against a timeline. In the second half of the twentieth century, Henry Gantt, a mechanical engineer, developed a chart that could be used as a visual tool to show scheduled and actual progress of large engineering projects, where an unanticpated resource overlap could have very serious financial consequences.

A Gantt chart shows immediately where there are overlapping project activities, enabling you to work out where there are any conflicts.

Using a Gantt Chart Simplify your project planning by using this system to check if there are any potential time conflicts in your schedule and to reschedule any overlapping activities.

Gantt Chart: Plot the Duration of each Activity

TASK	DAYS				
1.1	16	Interview customer focus group			
1.2	6		Write report		
2.1	6				Consult departments
	Days	5	10	15	20

How Many Days in a Year?

Remember that even a full-time member of a team will have a limited number of days to work on the project.

Number of days in the year	365
Less weekends	-104
Less national holidays	-8
Less annual leave	-24
Days available to work on the project	**229**

From the 229 working days you will also have to allow for sick leave and for the possibility of training days.

Get Agreement on Dates

Discuss the dates with the key people to make sure that they are really available at the time they are needed. If any team member has commitments in another part of the organization at the time when you will need her, work out a solution with her manager so that you can reschedule and avoid the conflicting dates. Good planning tends to avoid overlap because the problem reveals itself early enough for you to be able to do something about it. When someone is needed by more than one project at the same time, you may be able to help by assigning the tasks that do that do not require her specialist skills to someone else. If you know in advance that an overlap is going to occur, think about training someone else in the necessary skills so that you can avoid future bottlenecks.

A successful project is driven by a good schedule

TIP Ask team members to book their vacations as far in advance as they can, and use a year planner to plot vacations and identify any overlaps.

Summary: Planning the Project

Success with a project is as much to do with good planning as it is to do with bold action. Set tight objectives that can be measured by the value they will bring. Get a list of activities. Work out your resource requirements and make sure they are allocated to your project for the time they will be needed.

Bringing it All Together

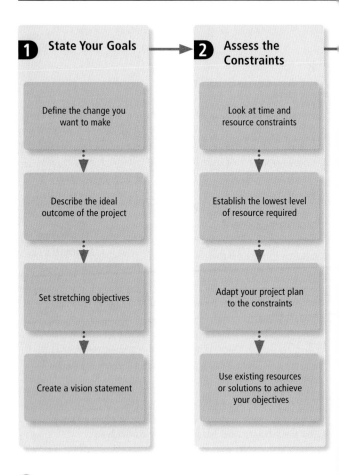

1 State Your Goals

Define the change you want to make

↓

Describe the ideal outcome of the project

↓

Set stretching objectives

↓

Create a vision statement

2 Assess the Constraints

Look at time and resource constraints

↓

Establish the lowest level of resource required

↓

Adapt your project plan to the constraints

↓

Use existing resources or solutions to achieve your objectives

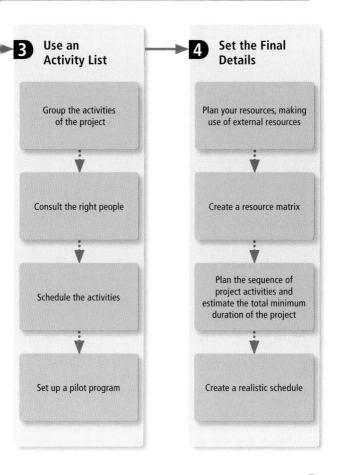

3 **Use an Activity List**

Group the activities of the project

↓

Consult the right people

↓

Schedule the activities

↓

Set up a pilot program

4 **Set the Final Details**

Plan your resources, making use of external resources

↓

Create a resource matrix

↓

Plan the sequence of project activities and estimate the total minimum duration of the project

↓

Create a realistic schedule

Validate the Plan

All well constructed plans have at least one thing in common—they all come up against unexpected and changing circumstances. Work with your team and other stakeholders to anticipate and preempt problems.

Identify Possible Threats

Ask your team to look at the schedule of activities and brainstorm a list of potential threats and problems that could prevent the straightforward implementation of the plan and interfere with the success of the project. Analyze the impact of each of the threats, then deal with each one individually, starting with those that would have the greatest impact on the project. Threats to activities that are on the project's critical path are usually the most dangerous. Draw up a contingency plan to deal with those threats that cannot be preempted.

Preempt Problems

For each threat on the list, ask yourself what you could do to reduce the probability that the problem will arise. Here are some examples of potential problems with suggestions for preemptive action:

POTENTIAL PROBLEM	PRE-EMPTIVE ACTION
Poor weather delays outside work	• Change the timing of the work schedule • Make sure that indoor work is also available for the people involved
Key materials are known to be in short supply	• Buy them earlier than is required • Substitute them with other materials
Trade unions may object to new ways of working	• Involve the unions and their members early in the project so that they are aware of what is going to happen
A key person is promoted out of the team	• Train a replacement in anticipation • Identify a substitute for each key person

think
SMART

Cultivate people in your organization who can provide the resources you need. If you're concerned that resources that have been promised may not arrive when they are needed try to preempt this eventuality with the managers of the resources in question.

Talk to the appropriate managers at a social function or over lunch and show your appreciation that they have agreed to supply the resource. Make sure that they understand what the benefit is to them. Tell them about other managers who have caused problems by letting project managers down. Your goal is to ensure that if they have to let someone down, the last person they will think about doing it to is you.

Make a Contingency Plan

For those threats that the team cannot find a way of preempting, consider a contingency plan. A contingency plan strives to minimize the damage that the problem will cause to the project. If the project needs a new piece of software, for example, look at what you would do if the software were delivered late. You may have to employ a contingency system and that may add to the costs.

Complete the Project Plan

Using the list of threats, the discussions on preempting problems, and the contingency plan, make the necessary changes to the plan. The team has its starting point and understands the result of the implementation of the plan. The project planning process never ends, so prepare the team for alterations as problems surface.

> **It isn't that they can't see the solution. It is that they can't see the problem.**
>
> G.K. Chesterton

Implement the Plan 3

The implementation of a good plan requires the right team. When the team sets out it needs to be aware of the problems that it may encounter as the project progresses. This chapter shows you how to:

- Define the roles and responsibilities of the members of your team
- Make a positive start to the project
- Predict and manage the risks inherent in any complex exercise
- Communicate with all the necessary people clearly and appropriately

Define the Project Roles

As project manager you have overall responsibility for the successful implementation of the plan. Get familiar with your responsibilities, think about being a leader, and make an honest assessment of your capabilities.

What are You Responsible For?

A successful project manager is both a manager and a team leader. Having completed the planning process and gained agreement to the resources you will need, you must now translate the plan into action. This involves selecting the right people for the team, focusing and motivating them to achieve the project goals, and helping them to develop as individuals and as team members. You will need to continue to develop good relationships with the project stakeholders and your sponsor. You will have to run efficient team meetings, administrate and coordinate, and communicate clearly to stakeholders at all levels at every step along the way.

Show Leadership The members of your team will look to you for leadership. Remember that they will take the lead from your enthusiasm and confidence.

Assess Yourself

So, do you have what it takes to be a leader? If you are not sure, ask someone whose opinion you respect if he would be happy to work in a team led by you. Once you have a good understanding of your strengths and weaknesses as a manager and leader you can develop the skills you lack through training and experience. Recognize that your role will be different from that of your team members. You are unlikely to be a technical or functional expert, and your primary role will be that of managing and motivating.

Define Your Role

Select your final team and allocate roles and responsibilities

⬇

Launch the project successfully and with a flourish

⬇

Motivate your team and focus it on the objectives of the project

⬇

Organize information systems

⬇

Organize information flow of the key facts to the key people

TECHNIQUES *to* practice

Motivation and leadership skills are key attributes of any successful manager.
The key to improving your skills is to think about how you are leading and motivating people in any environment. You can practice these skills outside your work environment by giving your time to help in the running of other organizations. You could, for example:

- Take responsibility for some aspect of a social club such as a tennis club and try to get the agreement of the members to your ideas.
- Help to run the local youth club and learn how to motivate young people who may be difficult.
- Work on motivating your own children into doing their least favorite tasks.

Assess People's Availability

Make a list of people who are right for the project and find out if they are available when you need them. Some of them may work in other areas in the organization, so you will need to negotiate their availability with their managers. Where several projects are under way at the same time you may have to negotiate with whoever is coordinating the use of resources across projects. As well as ensuring that people have the right skills, check that they will be willing and enthusiastic members

Every good team has a good team spirit

of the team. It is much easier to motivate people who like the objectives of the project and are excited to work on it.

Choose the Right People

Build your team carefully, bearing in mind that it is usually the people involved who make or break a project. When you have found someone with the right skills, ask yourself:

→ Do I know this person well enough to trust him?
→ Will I be able to work comfortably with him?
→ Will he get along with other members of the team?
→ Does he have all the skills needed or will I have to organize training for him?

A negative answer to any of these should make you question whether the individual is going to make the contribution that you require of him, even if he has the necessary skills and capabilities. If you do not know enough about someone to answer the questions, speak to another manager who knows him better.

Key Team Roles

ROLE	RESPONSIBILITY
Coordinator	Pulls together the work of the team as a whole
Critic	Monitors standards and analyzes the team's effectiveness
Ideas person	Encourages the team's innovative enthusiasm
Implementer	Ensures the smooth running of the team's activities and monitors its progress
External contact	Looks after the team's external contacts and looks for ideas from outside the project
Team builder	Helps with developing team spirit

Consider Team Roles

To operate efficiently you will need people to perform the roles of coordinator, critic, ideas person, implementer, external contact, and team builder. Most team members will fit well into one or more of these roles. You need them all. If, for example, you see that no one is challenging the team's standards, quality, and way of working, then you lack a critic. Keep challenging the team yourself until you see someone else leaning toward this role; then you can encourage him to do it. Discussing these roles openly with the team is a good way of building team spirit.

Recruit New Team Members

When you are choosing people to join the project team, remember that internal promotions have three distinct advantages over external recruitment:
- Internal promotion is cheaper
- Internal promotion reminds everyone that there is scope to improve their situation
- Internal recruits know the organization and can get started on the project more quickly.

It is important to sit down with each team member, internally promoted or not, to talk to them about their experience of different methods and processes.

Start Positively

Once you have the right people on board, you need to launch the project positively, so get the team off to a good start. Encourage everyone to come to an informal gathering to mark the start of the project.

Make an Active Start

At an early stage bring together the whole team for an interactive session that will probably take more than half a day. Let them know exactly what the project is about, explain what the targets are, and go through the SPRINT summary. Make sure everyone

> **Milestones measure the progress of a project**

knows how the project will benefit the organization, the team, and the individual members. Establish ground rules for sharing information and decision making. Ask your sponsor to attend at least part of the meeting so that he can greet each team member individually and emphasize the importance to the organization of the team's activities. Finish the meeting with refreshments so that people can get to know other members of the team.

Formalize the Project

Write a simple start-up report that everyone can sign off on. Make sure that you keep it free of jargon and unnecessarily complex language. Circulate it widely and encourage recipients of the report to give you feedback and suggestions; you may want to do this informally with a few key stakeholders before circulating it more widely. Use the report to show the importance of communication to the achievement of the objectives of the project.

There are two golden rules for an orchestra: start together and end together.

Thomas Beecham

Write a Start-Up Report

A start-up report should make everyone aware of the vision that has inspired the project. It should detail the measures of success the team will be aiming for, and the risks to the project that the team has identified.

Document all the resources that will be involved and name all the stakeholders so that everyone knows who they are. Give the document added credibility by asking the key people to sign the document. The report should contain the following information:

Vision Overall aim of the project	→ Show why the project has been initiated and what it is setting out to achieve → Spell out the benefits of the successful completion of the project at all levels
Targets Summary of key indicators, current performance, and target figures	→ Provide clear information about how the success of the project will be measured → Explain what business results should have been achieved by the time the project comes to an end
Milestones	→ Summarize the milestones so that everyone knows when they will have to deliver results
Risks and opportunities A list of potential risks and additional opportunities	→ Explain the threats that the team will have to avoid → Show other areas where improvements might be made to gain even greater benefit from the project
List of stakeholders	→ Name all interested parties, detailing their previous experience to add credibility to the team → List your customers and what they will gain from the project

Manage Risks

Even with the best-planned projects, something will go wrong. Unexpected events can threaten an important objective. Identify the critical ones in advance and assess their significance to the success of the project.

Identify Risks

Brainstorm with your team to identify risks that would threaten or delay the whole project. Start with actions that are on the critical path.

- **Expert resources**—Will they fit in with the team and accept the team's way of working or will they force the team to operate differently?
- **Unique resources**—Will they be available? Are they engaged on another project that might slip and need them to stay on for longer?
- **Customer requirements**—Could a new customer insight change what they want from the project?
- **Test equipment**—Will it be available and is it guaranteed to be reliable in the new environment of your project?

Be Prepared Make sure you have everything ready and functioning properly with the most recent information available before delegates arrive for a meeting.

- **Assumptions**—Go through the project plan carefully and look for areas where you have made assumptions. Each assumption that you make is a potential area of vulnerability.

The list of risks generated will be your risk register. Review this register regularly, particularly when you have made a major change to any part of a project.

Assess Probability and Impact

To determine the level of threat posed by any risk, look at the probability that it will occur and the impact that it would have on the project. Look also at the documentation of previous projects, including the risk registers, then identify similar areas of risk in your project.

5 minute FIX

If you are managing a crisis project and do not have enough time to do a full risk analysis, isolate those risks that are the most critical:

- Use the critical path analysis to identify the limited number of activity groups you are going to assess.

- Mark the probability and impact against each one; but move on as soon as you assess any risk as having a probability that is less than high.

Register of Risks

List the risks in order, giving precedence to risks that have a high probability of occurrence and will have a high impact on the project. This is the input document to the plan for how you are going to minimize the threat to the project carried by each eventuality listed on the register of risks.

Activity group	Identify the group that will be affected by the risk.
Risk	What is the risk? What might occur that would affect this activity group?
Probability that the risk will occur	High, medium, or low
Impact on project objectives	High, medium, or low

Agree Actions

Focusing first on the high probability/high impact risks, work with your team to identify mitigating actions. Ask yourself what preventive actions you could take to protect the activity group and the project.

Suppose, for example, that you are responsible for an activity group that includes an important training course aimed at training people to use a new system. Previous experience with these users suggests a high probability risk that they will reject the trainer's approach and the concepts he presents. The impact will be dramatic.

> **Uncontrolled risks can cause a project to go out of control**

- Identify some users who are likely to accept the training and some who will not.
- Bring them together as a representative group to participate in a pilot scheme.
- Establish contingency plans to reduce the impact on the project should the risk occur.

Review the Risk Status

Maintaining an overview of the risks that might threaten the project is critical to its success or failure. You will need to establish a simple system that will make it immediately apparent where the high risk areas are. Allocate a colored indicator to each of the risks on the risk register.

- Green indicates that you believe that the planned actions and contingency measures have more or less removed the risk in question.
- Yellow shows that the risk could still cause serious problems unless action is taken.
- Red shows that the actions that can be taken to reduce the probability of occurrence still leave a reasonable chance that the risk will occur, and that implementing the contingency plan will not protect the project from serious delay or disruption.

Are You in Control of Project Risks?

Allocate time at regular meetings to review the risk register, focusing on those risks that are still marked red. These are the risks that pose the greatest danger.

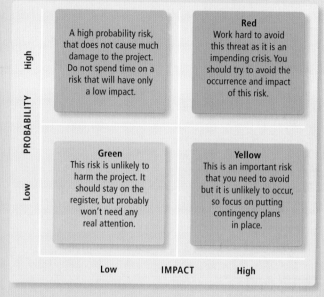

	Low ← IMPACT → **High**
High (PROBABILITY)	A high probability risk, that does not cause much damage to the project. Do not spend time on a risk that will have only a low impact.	**Red** Work hard to avoid this threat as it is an impending crisis. You should try to avoid the occurrence and impact of this risk.
Low	**Green** This risk is unlikely to harm the project. It should stay on the register, but probably won't need any real attention.	**Yellow** This is an important risk that you need to avoid but it is unlikely to occur, so focus on putting contingency plans in place.

Assess the Risks Everyone involved in the project needs to be aware of the risks that threaten it and to agree on the level of threat posed in each case.

Make Critical Decisions

As the project proceeds some activities will go according to plan and some will not. High quality decision making is vital. A decision is much more likely to be willingly implemented if the team is involved in making it.

Define the Ideal

First the team must agree on the criteria it will use to make the decision and list these, noting the ideal against each criterion. Suppose, for example, that you are deciding which of two potential suppliers to the project you should use. Ask the team to brainstorm what an ideal solution would look like, identifying the most important criteria. Three or four will probably stand out from the others. Now measure all the options against the ideal agreed for each

Make V-SAFE decisions

A wrong decision can have serious consequences for a project. Make a final validation of a decision using V-SAFE:

→ **Value**—Which decision is likely to have the most beneficial impact in meeting project objectives?
→ **Suitability**—Is the decision the most suitable one, given the current state of the project?
→ **Acceptability**—Is the decision acceptable to all the interested parties?
→ **Feasibility**—Will it be practical and feasible to implement the decision, given the constraints of time, resource, and budget on the project?
→ **Endurance**—Will the solution endure to the end of the project and into the future?

A negative response to any of these questions means that you are making a decision that carries some risk to the project, and you will have to reexamine it.

criterion. If at the end of the exercise two options have little to distinguish them, choose the one that you believe will be most acceptable to your sponsor and other stakeholders.

Get them Involved Decision making can be fun—people who are behind the project will make better decisions.

Practice Decision-Making

Decision-making is not confined to the workplace but is a skill that you can practice in everyday life. For example, if your social club is deciding where to hold its annual party, or the family is trying to make up its mind where to take its summer vacation:

- Get the interested parties together
- Make sure that everyone involved understands what is being proposed
- Ask them the five V-SAFE questions
- If the option meets V-SAFE criteria agree on the decision
- Search for other options if it fails.

When you have worked your way through the process, and particularly after you have taken people through the V-SAFE criteria, it is very likely that right decision in the situation will become obvious to everyone.

Summary: Getting Started

Get the implementation off to a flying start by getting the team and stakeholders together. Allocate their project roles to team members and make sure they have the skills to carry them out. Use a process for assessing and mitigating the risks involved in implementation, and get agreement to a logical process for making important decisions.

Taking the First Steps

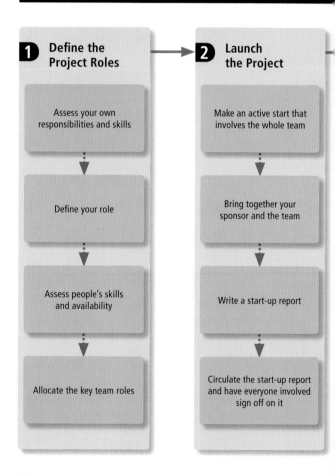

1 Define the Project Roles

Assess your own responsibilities and skills

Define your role

Assess people's skills and availability

Allocate the key team roles

2 Launch the Project

Make an active start that involves the whole team

Bring together your sponsor and the team

Write a start-up report

Circulate the start-up report and have everyone involved sign off on it

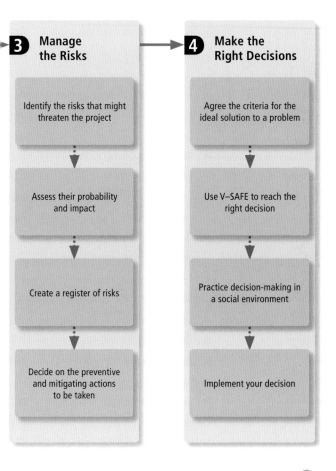

3 Manage the Risks

Identify the risks that might threaten the project

⬇

Assess their probability and impact

⬇

Create a register of risks

⬇

Decide on the preventive and mitigating actions to be taken

4 Make the Right Decisions

Agree the criteria for the ideal solution to a problem

⬇

Use V–SAFE to reach the right decision

⬇

Practice decision-making in a social environment

⬇

Implement your decision

Communicate Clearly

Knowledge must be made available to the people who need it when and where they need it. Your challenge as project manager is to encourage communication between team members and facilitate the exchange of knowledge.

Manage Information

Everyone must have easy access to key project information whenever they need it. Ensure that all the project data is up to date and recorded efficiently by setting up a knowledge center. Each item of information generated by the project should be regarded as potentially valuable, either to your own project or to those that come after. It will be obvious in most cases what needs to be stored, but try to think more widely. If, for example, a project involves researching a benchmark for productivity, this may be of interest to other parts of the organization.

Appoint a Coordinator

If the project has limited information you can probably manage it yourself. However, in a large project it will pay to put one person in charge. Team members will bring their progress reports, updates to the network diagram, Gantt charts, and activity reports to this coordinator.

Make the Best Use of Information

HIGH IMPACT

- Keeping notes of errors made during the project and learning lessons for future reference
- Making available an easy-to-use index of how the project data is to be stored
- Maintaining records of who has taken what out of the knowledge center

NEGATIVE IMPACT

- Removing information about any mistakes made
- Allowing team members to invent their own record system
- Keeping information at team members' work stations
- Failing to keep a record of where the key project information is at all times

Set up a Knowledge Center

A knowledge center is a central location where all the information required to run a project is gathered and communicated to those involved.

Some project managers set up a project "war room," where information is stored and made available. Here are the hard copy files, the schedules on the wall for discussion purposes, the manuals and journals the team is using, and terminals to access the electronically stored data. Make sure the focus of the information is on how the project is progressing. Classify the data:

→ **General planning information**—The vision statement, objectives, master schedule, and network diagram.

→ **General data**—Any background information that might be needed to carry out project activities.

→ **Completed activities**—Data gathered on finished activities.

→ **Activities in progress**—Data being gathered or made available to people carrying out activities.

→ **Activities not yet started**—Data that might be found useful at some time in the future.

Collate Information Make sure that all the information necessary to the smooth running of a project is collated together and that the data is integrated effectively.

Share Knowledge

Consider who needs what information, in what format, and when. Apart from the members of the project team there are others inside and outside the organization who stand to benefit from some of the information you can share. Think carefully about who needs to have access to what information—no one needs an information overload.

- Refer to the list of stakeholders in the start-up report to ensure that no one is forgotten.
- Concentrate on people whose access to information will be crucial to the project, but do not ignore others who may have less significant roles.
- Plan how you are going to make the information available, bearing in mind that generating and finding information should take as little time as possible.
- Make sure that your coordinator knows what the priorities are.
- Meet often with team members on a one-to-one basis to keep them informed of progress and keep you informed of what information they are generating and what information they need.

Case study: Listening Actively

Alan, a project manager for a banking group, noticed that Ben, a key team member, had been very quiet at the last review meeting, breaking his silence only to make a comment that showed he believed that a rival bank was doing much better in its treatment of small businesses. Alan asked Ben to meet him for lunch and asked some probing questions about how he felt. Ben confessed that he was thinking of leaving and joining the rival bank. Alan persuaded Ben to stay and help the bank to improve its treatment of small businesses.

- *Because he was listening so actively Alan was able to pick up on a small hint and kept a key member of the team on board.*
- *By encouraging Ben to communicate his views, and by being open to this source of information, Alan was able to improve the bank's service.*

Listen to Others

The ability to listen attentively and actively is a vital communication skill. Encourage team members to be open and honest with you. Keep an open mind and show that you will listen without prejudging what they have to say.

Listen Attentively
Always listen to people carefully, making good eye contact and giving the talker your full attention while they are speaking to you, even if you disagree with what they are saying.

Respond Actively
Have the relevant facts and information in front of you so that you can respond intelligently. Ask the speaker for clarification, if necessary. Note down key facts or points that require action.

Encourage Feedback
Watch the speaker's body language and respond appropriately: if the speaker is eager to talk, avoid interruptions; draw hesitant talkers into speaking by asking open questions.

Use Technology

Exploit technology to improve communication. Learn to use one of the various software packages that allow you to add a graph or chart to a computer-generated spreadsheet of figures to make them more instantly understandable and to accentuate the point the figures are illustrating.

Use Email Properly

Email is an extremely useful timesaving device when handled correctly. Remember that you receive as many emails as you send, which means that you should think twice before sending each message. Ask yourself:

- Is it absolutely vital to send this message now?
- Is email the most effective means of communication in this case given the current situation?

Send as few emails as you can to get the job done well and avoid checking your inbox constantly. Avoid hiding behind email, using it to ask difficult questions and make difficult demands of people electronically rather than in person. If you do this, people will dread opening your emails.

The quality of communication can make or break a project

Keep the Channels Open

HIGH IMPACT

- Using email as an adjunct to face-to-face and telephone communication
- Putting someone in charge of each forum discussion
- Replying quickly to every email even if only to acknowledge that you have received it and when you will deal with it

NEGATIVE IMPACT

- Limiting your communication with stakeholders to email only
- Starting a forum with initial enthusiasm but failing to appoint anyone to maintain it and keep it relevant and lively
- Not responding to emails, so that people don't know if you have received theirs

Audit the Project Events

TOPIC	COMMENTS	RESPONSES	POSTED BY/ DATE
Availability of Version 3 of new program	I have heard that Version 3 is late—by how long?		Office manager 6/24
Respond		Their salesman said it was on time	IT manager 6/25
		I know that testing was three months late but they may have caught up	IT assistant 6/27

Stay Interactive

Constant communication with stakeholders is key, and the most effective way of doing that is in face-to-face meetings. Increasingly, however, teams, particularly cross-functional teams, are in different locations, which makes getting together possible only on an occasional basis. Look to technology as a solution to this by using it to record discussions. Set up an online discussion forum for any relevant aspect of the project. Make sure that each forum has a clear purpose and that all the contributors have a shared goal. The forum will also provide an audit trail of key discussions and decisions so that, for example, a new team member or stakeholder can find out how a decision was made or what ground a discussion covered.

Virtual Conference A forum discussion keeps everyone up to date on the progress of a project. Those wishing to contribute press the Respond button under Topic to add their comments.

TIP Make sure that everyone is aware of the efforts the team is making to communicate to all the people it needs to keep informed.

4

Leading the Team

To achieve success in a project means getting the best out of the team of people responsible for achieving the objectives and milestones. The project manager must be able to lead a motivated and enthusiastic team effectively. This chapter explains how to:

- Vary your leadership style according to the circumstances
- Overcome people's natural resistance to changing how they operate
- Build a team environment that is continuously learning from its own experience and that of other people

Lead Effectively

There are many different styles of leadership. Projects rely on teamwork, so it is important to favor consensus building over a dictatorial approach. Be prepared to switch from one style to another when necessary.

Understand Leadership Styles

There is a spectrum of leadership styles, and you will need to adopt them all at certain points in the project. Your style may usually be to seek consensus, but if the project is about to miss a milestone you may have to tell people what to do in order to correct the problem. Your predominant style will depend to some extent on the culture of your organization, the nature and time frame of the project, the characteristics of the team, and your own personality. If your approach isn't getting the results you need, try changing your leadership style until you hit on one that works in the situation. If your team or some members of the team have been displaying a lack of interest or enthusiasm about the project, this may be all that is required to reignite the spark.

Inspire Your Team The importance of the quality of your leadership cannot be overstated—an inspiring leader will galvanize her team into positive action.

Choose a Leadership Style

A good leader understands what motivates her team and recognizes which style of leadership is appropriate in any given circumstances; but there are some guidelines for when different styles might be adopted.

→ **Dictatorial**—Making decisions alone and being autocratic may be appropriate if the project is facing a crisis and there is no time for consultation. However, since it discourages teamwork, the dictatorial style should be used sparingly. To use this style effectively you must have all the information you need and have the respect of the team.

→ **Analytical**—Making a decision based on all the available facts may be appropriate when the project is under time pressure or threat and the right decision must be made quickly. This is still an autocratic style, but the team members feel involved because they will have been asked to provide the facts on which the decision is based.

→ **Opinion-seeking**—Asking the team for opinions prior to making a decision builds team confidence and shows that you value people's opinions.

→ **Democratic**—Encouraging team participation and involvement in decision making is an essential style that should be used on a regular basis. It empowers team members and helps to strengthen their commitment to the project. Remember that consensus does not necessarily mean that everyone agrees with the decision, but that everyone on the team will commit to the decision of the team.

5 minute FIX

Take a few minutes in the second month of the project to get feedback on your leadership style:

- Ask two of the key team members to comment on how your leadership style could be improved.
- Do the same with your manager.

Get Results

Two major factors that you will have to take into account when deciding on your style of leadership are time constraints and people's commitment to the project:

- **Time**—If you are under heavy time pressure you may have no option but to use a dictatorial style; you need action fast and do not have the luxury of time to involve the team in decision making.
- **Commitment**—If you want to gain commitment to the project, you must involve others in the key decisions to increase their enthusiasm to implement the decision.

The goal is to make the right decision and set the team on the right path. Do not expect the team to do everything in exactly the way that you would do it, if they are producing good results. You even have to allow people to make mistakes if by doing so they learn and start to produce better results. If you always step in to prevent a decision that you know is not in the best interests of the project, you will not allow your people to grow and develop. People learn a lot from their mistakes. Use your discretion about when to step back and let them make mistakes.

Use conflict constructively to encourage healthy competition

think SMART

When two people get into conflict they each stop being able to see the other person's point of view. You will need to do something to ease the deadlock.

Suggest to each of the people involved that they produce a quick two-point defense of the opposite point of view, then ask if they can reach a compromise position together, based on their new-found objectivity.

Exercise Good Leadership

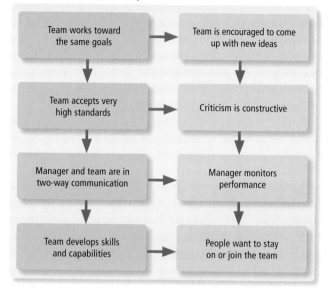

Team works toward the same goals	→ Team is encouraged to come up with new ideas
↓	↓
Team accepts very high standards	→ Criticism is constructive
↓	↓
Manager and team are in two-way communication	→ Manager monitors performance
↓	↓
Team develops skills and capabilities	→ People want to stay on or join the team

Resolve Conflict

Clashes of personality and differences of opinion are inevitable when a group of people work together for a period of time. Disputes may arise from the fact that people have different standards of work, or because some team members simply do not get along. When team members are in disagreement you must find a way of resolving the conflict, either by stepping in and making a decision yourself, or by talking to the people concerned, individually or together. If you believe that conflict is threatening the success of the project, then that is the time to become assertive. Conflicts sometimes arise from scheduling, where one team member might want more time for an activity that a colleague thinks could be done faster. Work through the schedule with them to arrive at a solution that suits everyone.

Keep People on Board A team that is plainly enjoying its work is the one that people will stay on and that others will want to join. It's up to you to make sure that the team members remain enthusiastic and committed.

Develop Your Team

It is important to recognize that at the start of any project all teams behave in the same way. It is up to you to make sure that people feel comfortable and that they belong to a team that is enthusiastic about the project.

Listen carefully to what people are saying and how they are saying it so that you can detect how they feel about their part in the project. These are the stages that all teams go through:

→ **Forming**—When they first come together people are anxious about what is expected of them. Make sure that roles and responsibilities are clear and leave no room for doubt about what is expected from each person.

→ **Storming**—This is the most precarious stage in the team development process. Members will try to assert their positions and jockey for seniority and authority over others. Make it abundantly clear that teamwork is crucial to the success of the project and that people are dependent on each other.

→ **Norming**—During this phase the systems and processes that will strengthen the way the team operates start to fall into place. Get everyone's agreement on using these working practices and develop the team's skills in carrying them out.

→ **Performing**—The team members start to work positively and productively and become encouraging and supportive of their colleagues. Build the team's confidence in its collective ability and keep the team members focused on completing the project and achieving the objectives.

If you learn to recognize the stages of development that people are going through you will be able to create the right atmosphere for the efficient management of the project.

TIP **As project manager, you must be sure to be fair to everyone. If you show any favoritism at all it may lead to dissent among the members of the team.**

Encourage Teamwork

For a team to be successful, people must learn to pull together. Encourage teamwork by promoting a positive atmosphere in which people compete with their ideas rather than with their personalities and egos. Talk about each person's strengths and contribution to the team and encourage the team members to appreciate what others are doing. Praise them as a team as well as individually, so that everyone feels like part of a team where the whole is greater than the sum of all its parts.

Understand Team Development

The job of the project manager is to take team members as quickly as possible to the stage at which they are working together and getting results. Use your authority and example to defuse any conflict and put a stop to early political maneuvering by showing that it will be ineffective. Some people will be more committed to the project than others. It can be tempting to spend more time with the enthusiastic people, when actually you would spend your time better talking to the doubters about the benefits of the project to the organization, the team, and the individual team members.

Coordinate the Team
It can be difficult to get everyone to pull together. Promote good teamwork by emphasizing the vital importance of cooperation.

Overcome Resistance to Change

People get very used to a set way of doing things and do not welcome being asked to behave differently. Good leaders will overcome this resistance, persuading people to accept that nothing stays the same forever.

Communicate Change

While some people will embrace change, most people approach it with a certain amount of caution. The key to overcoming this natural resistance is to involve people in the forthcoming change as early as possible. Explain that there are going to be some changes; but ask for their opinion and look for feedback. You are dealing with experienced people who will probably have valuable insights into the best way to operate. If, for example, you are responsible for installing new checkouts in a supermarket, you will court disaster if you don't involve checkout clerks at an early stage. If you leave it until the terminals are installed, you are unlikely to achieve your objectives. Ask for a number of representative checkout clerks to look at the new equipment at an early stage in the project and give their opinions of it.

think
SMART

Do not discount the role of personal motivating factors. When people are looking at the possibility of change they are not thinking, "What is in it for the organization?" but "What is in it for me?" (WIIFM).

While people work for the benefit of the organization, they live for themselves and they will be better motivated if they feel that they are also producing a result for themselves. Whenever you make a presentation or discuss your project with other people, make sure that you are answering the WIIFM question, whether they ask it openly or not.

Use Agents of Change

The biggest influence you can bring to bear to overcome resistance is the peer group. You will find key opinion leaders in every part of an organization, so when you plan for overcoming resistance to change, look for these people and make sure that they are firmly on board and supportive of the change you are introducing. They are your agents of change. Get them to be part of the pilot study so that they can advocate the change from a position of knowledge and experience. Include them in your communications plan so that they can take up their role of persuading people that the project is a good idea, not only for the organization but for them.

The Four Stages of Change
Recognize that people go through four stages, starting out wary of change and finishing up welcoming it.

Handle the Stages of Resistance to Change

DENIAL	"This change will never happen."
RESISTANCE	"Well, even if it does, I'm not going to change what I do."
EXPLORATION	"Perhaps this isn't so bad; there may be something in it for me."
COMMITMENT	"I can't understand why we didn't always do it this way."

TIP If at least 20 percent of the people who need to change are themselves agents of change the process of change will probably go quite smoothly.

Learn Continuously

When an experienced employee leaves an organization, her skills and knowledge go with her and are lost, unless the organization has thought seriously about learning continuously from her beforehand.

Learn Across the Functions

In order to avoid repeating mistakes or duplicating effort it is vital that individuals and teams learn from each other. One of the most effective ways of learning and transferring knowledge is giving people the opportunity to work together on cross-functional teams. Another project team in another department may have skills and experience that would help you to take a short cut to a particular milestone. Take a look at your project plan and decide where you could learn from other departments or projects and who could learn from you. Then set up a forum to make the knowledge transfer happen. Pull the appropriate people together to address a particular issue, then document what has been learned and make it available to other teams and individuals with an interest in that issue. If, for example, your project will need to use a particular piece of engineering software, find out who else is using it at the moment or will need to use it in the future and set up a cross-functional user group.

Make the Best Use of a Retreat

HIGH IMPACT

- Project managers attending retreats with the team to learn from the team
- Making it in the best interests of people to learn and seek improvement
- Looking for root cause and fixing real problems

NEGATIVE IMPACT

- Project managers attending retreats so that the team can learn from them
- Allowing people to end up in a situation where they are too busy to think
- Allowing a temporary "quick fix" to become a long-term solution

Use Thinking Days

Most project team members are busy people with operational targets to hit. This gives them very little time to stop and think. Yet when they do take time out to reflect teams can come up with ideas that improve effectiveness and productivity. Many organizations are introducing regular activities of this nature. Work out who should attend a retreat or thinking day. You may want the cross-functional group to look for innovative ways to change; or you may simply want to take time to reflect on past events and how things could be improved in the future. The key is to provide a quiet and creative environment, without any interruptions.

Tap into the Energy The calm, reflective atmosphere of a retreat can produce more creativity than a series of in-house meetings.

5 minute FIX

Today's work environment requires people to turn up to do the job they did yesterday and to improve the way that it will be done tomorrow.

- Take advantage of the creative environment of a thinking day to ask each of your team members to think of one way in which they could improve their future performance.

- Ask them to put it into practice the following week and note the results.

Check for Cause and Effect

The key driver for problem solving and learning is persuading people to think about cause and effect and move toward addressing the cause of a problem rather than the effect. Take a simple household example. Your washing machine is leaking. The cause is obvious—a hose has frayed and has a slight leak. You decide the leak is very small and put a bowl under the hose. Your decision is aimed at the effect. It has solved the problem quickly and with little effort. However, if you are to prevent the leak getting so bad that the hose bursts, causing a flood, you will have to find a solution to the cause of the problem.

- If something goes wrong take some time to identify the root cause of the problem.
- Once you have identified the root cause and found a preferred solution, think about what other aspect of the project could benefit from a similar fix.

Use PERL (Plan, Execute, Reflect, Learn)

PERL is a tool that helps teams think about continuous improvement and learning. It gives a structure to a retreat or a regular meeting of the project team. You may also find it useful to use the process when an important milestone has been achieved.

- **Plan**—What is the plan? What are the activities in the plan, and what are the time lines?
- **Execute**—Focusing on the objectives of the exercise, implement the plan.

The PERL Cycle looks at any activity or project in a logical fashion and ensures that individuals and teams not only plan properly and execute the plan effectively but also that they learn from their experience.

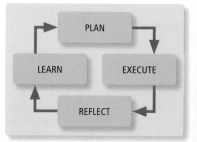

Case study: Fixing the Cause

Beryl was the managing director of a company based in the US that sold complex electronic instruments. On a trip to Europe, she went to one of her factories and was surprised to find that they were spraying black paint on the insides of the cabinets of their products. When she asked Bill, the factory manager, why, he responded that while the cabinet met the electronic interference regulations of the US it failed to comply with European rules. Beryl insisted that their customers be nofitied of a short delay in delivery while the reason why the instrument was radiating interference was investigated. Within two weeks the problem had been located and fixed.

• By identifying the cause of the problem Beryl was able to reduce future costs by cutting out the need for paint spraying.
• She had allowed the whole company to learn more about electronic interference and how it could be avoided.

- **Reflect**—Assess the implications of the activities you carried out and think about how you could have improved any aspect of the implementation. Look for the root cause of any problems.
- **Learn**—Look at any procedures you might change as the result of the reflection stage in the process.

Perhaps the most important of these four words is "reflect." When things go wrong, reactive teams ask, "What are we going to do about this problem?" Reflective teams ask, "How should we change our planning so that it doesn't happen again?" If you and your team adopt the PERL-cycle principle, you will become more and more effective, and you will be well equipped to avoid recurring problems and the repetition of mistakes.

TIP **If you stop learning you will not stand still but will simply become less and less effective.**

Summary: Taking the Lead

A team that is well led is more powerful and effective than the sum of the abilities of its members. Plan the style of leadership you will use in different circumstances. Get the team working together so that it handles change willingly and is well motivated to get the job done. Learn from everything the team does and record that learning.

Dealing with Change and Conflict

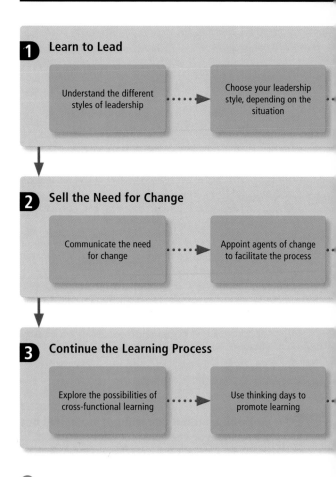

1 **Learn to Lead**

Understand the different styles of leadership

● ● ● ● ● ▶

Choose your leadership style, depending on the situation

2 **Sell the Need for Change**

Communicate the need for change

● ● ● ● ● ▶

Appoint agents of change to facilitate the process

3 **Continue the Learning Process**

Explore the possibilities of cross-functional learning

● ● ● ● ● ▶

Use thinking days to promote learning

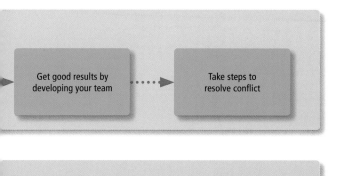

Get good results by developing your team ┄┄┄▶ Take steps to resolve conflict

Learn to handle the four stages of resistance to change ┄┄┄▶ Encourage people to consider how change will benefit the organization

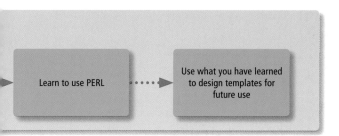

Learn to use PERL ┄┄┄▶ Use what you have learned to design templates for future use

Monitor Progress 5

The key to successful implementation of a plan is being in control. You will need a feedback system that tells you what is going right and what is going wrong. A system of key indicators allows you to be in control of the project and reach a successful conclusion. This chapter shows you how to:

- Track your progress throughout the project
- Hold effective review meetings
- Maximize the impact of the project
- Establish the right work/life balance so that you will bring a positive mental attitude to all of your projects

Track Progress

Keep control of your project by managing your plan so that it moves forward smoothly. Make sure that you set up a process that will highlight potential problems.

Monitor Effectively

Effective monitoring allows you to gather information that enables you to measure your progress against your original plan and make necessary adjustments in time to avoid real disruption to the plan. You will need to monitor external issues that are important to the success of the project, especially those that are drivers of the project.

Monitor Your Plan

If your plan is to succeed, it will need constant review. Key elements of every plan should be monitored to provide an insight into different perspectives:
- **Customers**—Are we delivering the project objectives?
- **Sponsor**—Are we on track, on time, within budget?
- **Team**—Are the team members still motivated and aligned to the project goals?
- **Suppliers**—Are there any critical bottlenecks with the delivery of supplies?

Anyone responsible for an activity must report progress.

Relate to External Suppliers Effectively

HIGH IMPACT

- Realizing that they can be a threat since you do not have control over their activities
- Making them feel part of the team by inviting them to meetings and gatherings
- Tracking their progress in the same way as you track the progress of the project

NEGATIVE IMPACT

- Having no contact with them until they are due to deliver
- Being the only person to have contact with them
- Relying on them to keep you up to date on progress
- Believing that if you haven't heard from them, everything must be going well

Use Reports

Encourage the team to take reports seriously and to submit them on time. Reports should record the current state of the project, achievements since the last report, and potential problems or threats to milestones. As project manager you should review the reports and summarize the position for your sponsor and stakeholders. Having considered the importance of the issues raised in the reports, use a red, yellow, and green status system to help you to draw up your review meeting agenda, so that the most important items will take priority.

Understand the Monitoring Process

Team members prepare progress reports

Project manager summarizes reports

Plans are updated, if necessary

Periodic meetings are held to monitor milestones

Items are listed on the regular review meeting agenda

Prepare Frequent Reports

The more complex the project the more frequent should be the reports, as they may be your main source of information about various issues. Think about how often you will need to prepare progress reports and hold review meetings. You may require daily or weekly reports on a crucial activity on the critical path. When you are well into the project try reducing the frequency of reports and meetings or dramatically reducing the amount of time allocated to meetings; if nothing goes wrong, you are saving everyone's time. Do not take too large a risk—you don't want to put the project in jeopardy—but it is worth avoiding having meetings where there is little to discuss.

think
SMART

Tracking the progress of a project can take up a lot of time—why not free up some of your time by delegating some of the responsibility for checking with team members, and recording progress?

Delegate the tasks of evaluation to other team members on a rotating basis, with each person taking turns keeping track of them for the month between progress meetings. Ask the person responsible to write a short summary of any reports that are of relevance to the project and the team, highlighting areas that will need attention if the project is to stay on track.

Look for Visibility

Your meetings should reveal the things you need to know, and your key performance indicators should be the crucial indicators of success. Make sure that they give you visibility in the critically important areas of:

- **Performance**—Do they show progress toward the objectives of the project?
- **Plan**—Are the scheduled activities still the right ones, and are they on track and within budget?
- **People**—Is everyone on the team still motivated, and do they have the necessary skills and time to carry out their responsibilities on the project?
- **Problems**—Are issues and concerns being picked up and managed as early as possible?

> When all hands are on the wheel the project will keep moving

TIP When reviewing your key indicators imagine that you are your customer.

Take Control

As project manager, your job is to be in control of events. You should have a tracking system that works in the same way as the dashboard of a car, with accurate indicators of what is happening all the time, so that you can make adjustments as and when they are needed. Your tracking system should show you what has happened in the past and forecast how you will be doing in the future. Your indicators should tell you, for example, that if a downward trend in achieving time frames continues you are going to miss out on an important milestone or be late in hitting an objective. Look ahead constantly and aim to resolve concerns before they become crises. Do not ignore uncertainties—if you cannot be sure that a resource is going to be available to you at the time you need it, for example, plan accordingly so that you can deal with the situation. Whenever you do have to handle a crisis, take time out after the crisis has passed to reflect on what you could have done differently to prevent it from happening.

Customer-Focused Indicators

Some or all of your project's objectives will be concerned with your customers. Check with your customers that the objectives continue to reflect what they want and that you are putting effort into activities that will really help them.

→ Ask your customers whether there are any other areas in which your project could help them.
→ Look for any improvements to the project that you can make relatively easily but that will have a major positive impact on the service to your customers.

Sometimes a small change to a project plan can offer a significant benefit to a customer. Find out where that is the case by discussing your performance indicators with your customers.

Hold Review Meetings

Hold review meetings throughout the life of a project to discuss progress and milestones. Running these meetings efficiently is vital to maintaining their credibility; make sure that everyone is well prepared.

Plan a Review

Divide review meetings into two groups—regular reviews, held once a month to monitor the detail of activities, achievements, and issues in implementing the plan, and event-driven reviews, to which stakeholders such as your sponsor will be invited, held to mark milestones or to deal with a crisis. Milestone meetings are usually called to check on the business aspects of the project. The sponsor will simply be ascertaining that certain objectives are being met:

> **The meeting is a useful resource that should not be squandered**

- Is it staying within budget?
- Have the business benefits that should have occurred by now actually been achieved?
- Is the project on course to deliver the other business benefits that are listed as its objectives?

TECHNIQUES *to* practice

Take punctuality seriously. If one team member is ten minutes late for a meeting of six people that cannot start without him, he has wasted an hour of valuable working time.

- Set standards for punctuality at the outset—make it absolutely clear that it is not permissible to be late.
- Explain that you regard lack of punctuality as rude behavior that cannot be tolerated.
- Insist that someone who offends twice sends a personal note of apology to each of the other participants.

Invite the Right People

The key to selecting the right people to attend meetings is that they will all have a valid contribution to make. Your sponsor will need to attend some meetings but not all. It is likely that key team members will be present at every review. Call in other team members only when they are needed—their presence for the entire duration of the meeting may not be necessary. If you need a decision on something, make sure that the person who can make the decision is present and that you have all the information he will need. The key to inviting the right people is to choose those who will make a valid contribution. Avoid having people attend just because they have attended all the previous meetings, but understand that the absence of a particular team member may present a threat to the project. The overall aim is not to waste anyone's time.

Keep to the Point

Remind the review meeting of the objectives of the project. Check the project against the time line. If people stray from the point bring them back to it by saying, for example, "That could be an interesting discussion later, but let's get back to the main point of this meeting for now."

Chair a Review Meeting

The aim of a review is to keep people up to date with the project's progress so that everyone has a shared understanding of what is happening.

> Prepare an agenda, allocating time to each item

> Invite attendees and circulate the agenda

> Focus the team on appraisal, and aim for agreement on actions

TIP Ensure that you return to the objectives of the project during each meeting, identifying which have been achieved, and which remain.

Overcome Problems

Once you start to implement the plan in the real world problems will crop up. Encourage team members to raise concerns, and use the discipline of problem-solving techniques to tackle difficulties as they arise.

Raise Concerns

Your primary aim is to identify problems early enough to prevent them from becoming crises. It is far more difficult to take remedial action when a problem has become urgent. Although you may create extra work by examining some problems that do not actually arise, it is far better to err on the side of caution than to find that a problem has escalated into a crisis without your knowledge. With experience, the team will get better at judging when and whether to raise a concern.

Case study: Preempting Problems

Tom, a team member in a construction project, heard from a supplier's clerk that there was a chance that an important component, due in two months, might be delivered late. He reported this to his project manager, Bernie, who raised the concern with the supplier's managing director. The supplier told Bernie that he believed they still might make the planned delivery date and that Bernie's would be the first project to get the component.

• By raising the concern at an early stage, Tom made sure that their project was the least likely to suffer if there were a delay.
• By realizing that there could, nevertheless, be a problem, Bernie was able to look at a contingency plan if the delivery were to be late.

TIP Ask team members to suggest solutions to any problems they raise so that some problem-solving work has been done before you are involved.

Update the Plan

Once a concern has been raised and a team member has agreed to carry out problem-solving activities,

Enjoy the challenge Every challenge you overcome in life will be a learning experience that will teach you to anticipate problems and how best to tackle them.

record this. Make sure that the problem-solving process includes the briefing of the knowledge coordinator. Ask the coordinator to document ongoing problem-solving activities as "open items." Assess all open items at your regular review meetings using a simple red, yellow, and green classification. Recognize that major issues may require a significant change to the plan.

Use the Four Ps

A useful problem-solving technique is to hone in on four areas—the Four Ps—to find out what is causing the difficulty. For example, if production is falling short of target, consider which of the following is the culprit:

- **People**—Do people have the right skills and support?
- **Product**—Is there something wrong in the design of the product or the production method?
- **Process**—Would an improvement in one of our business processes cure the problem?
- **Procurement**—Does it have something to do with the products and services that we buy?

Deal with Change

Change is inevitable in any project. A customer will change his mind about a requirement, a senior manager will change the focus. You must be able to negotiate change, adapt the plan, and keep everyone up to date.

Understand Change

Some changes will be within your control, such as shortening the schedule because activities are being completed more quickly as you work through the plan. Other changes will be imposed upon you, such as when a customer asks for something different, or a superior decides to reassign two of your key people to another job. Alternatively, your monitoring system may have highlighted the need for a change to avoid a potential problem or threat. Whenever the need for change arises, it is vital to be able to adjust the project plan. You must also be able to measure whether the change that you have made has had the desired effect. When it happens, bring the team together to evaluate how the changes may affect the original objectives of the project.

> **You can't think your way out of a box, you've got to act.**
>
> Tom Peters

think SMART

When an event occurs that seriously interrupts the project, the shock to the team can lead to a drop in morale and motivation as the team realizes that it will not bring what it has been doing to completion.

Inform some key members about the event first. That way when the rest of the team is told, these key members can help you to encourage the team to treat the altered circumstances positively and start discussing the way forward.

Assess the Impact of Change

Before you commit to making any changes, assess their impact on the project. Suppose a key team member in a research project has been recruited by a competitor and has immediately stopped working on your project. You will have to address:

- **Time frame**—By the time you have replaced the individual and the new person has been brought up to speed, you may find that some of the activities will have slipped. If these activities were on the critical path the whole time frame of the project will be threatened and you will have to get it back on track
- **Budget**—You will have to recruit a replacement, possibly using temporary staff to fill the gap
- **Order of activities**—You will probably have to revise the network diagram to take account of the new situation
- **People**—There may be an impact on the morale of the team, and other team members may leave the team.

Look at all the alternatives before changing a major component of the plan. Examine the alternatives with the team, decide on the changes you are going to make, document them on the original plan, and gain approval for the changes to the plan from your sponsor and other interested parties.

Tackle Change Effectively

Discuss the impact of a change with the team

If a change has a major impact look at alternatives

Inform everyone of the project changes as soon as possible

Seek approval from stakeholders and superiors

Implement the change

Maximize Impact

As a project draws to its close, it is important to evaluate exactly what can be learned for the next time. Take your project through a formal close-down process that ties up all the loose ends and celebrates its success.

See Projects Through

Inevitably, toward the end of a project, some team members will start to move on to other assignments. It is important to keep the remaining team members focused on final objectives until the very end of the project when you write a formal close-down report and hold a final meeting. You may have to protect your resources from being moved off the project too early, particularly if the most significant objective has been achieved. Avoid an untidy end with compromises being made on some of the minor objectives and some benefits dissipated because final activities are rushed or haphazard.

End on a High Note

Make sure that all members of the team go their separate ways feeling as positive as possible, especially since you may want to work with the same people on subsequent projects. Indeed, keep up your good relationships with all the stakeholders. Thank everyone individually. Hold a final meeting where your sponsor can thank the team and confirm that the project has indeed brought benefits. Compile a close-down report. Mark the end of the project with a celebration in recognition of the team's hard work.

A positive ending will lead to success in the future

TIP Publicize the achievements of the team and mention the key contributors by name.

End a Project Properly

A close-down report is an excellent and effective way to celebrate the team's successful completion of the project and is a good jumping-off point for the next project.

→ Evaluate the achievement of the project's objectives.
→ Assess the use of resources throughout the project.
→ Bring any lessons learned to future projects.

Close-Down Report

PARTS OF REPORT	CONTENT	PURPOSE
Performance indicators	A comparison of what the project has achieved against its original stated targets	1 Explains the reasons for any variations between targets and actual achievements 2 Validates the original investment appraisal
Resource utilization	An assessment of the resources planned and those that were used	1 States why the project used more or fewer resources than planned 2 Validates the budget allocated to the project
Strengths and weaknesses	An appraisal of what went well with the project and what went wrong or caused problems or difficulties	1 Includes input from the team to make sure all possible lessons were learned 2 Makes sure that the others can learn from this project
Success factors	A record of the top ten factors judged to be critical to the success of your project	1 Lists the factors that created your success, as seen by all stakeholders and team members 2 Creates a list that will provide valuable information for future project managers

Summary: Tracking Your Progress

You cannot achieve success unless you have tight control of your progress to date. Put in place a tracking system that measures where you are in the plan and anticipates problems. Hold effective review meetings and overcome problems as you hit them. Finish with a flourish by making sure that the project has achieved its objectives.

Keeping Things under Control

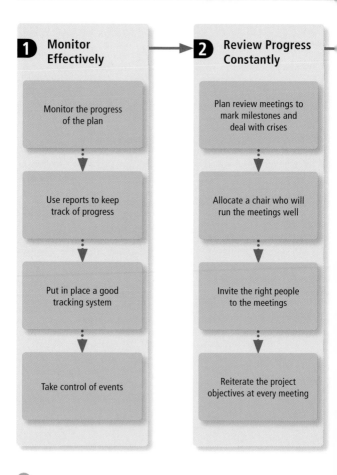

1 Monitor Effectively

Monitor the progress of the plan

Use reports to keep track of progress

Put in place a good tracking system

Take control of events

2 Review Progress Constantly

Plan review meetings to mark milestones and deal with crises

Allocate a chair who will run the meetings well

Invite the right people to the meetings

Reiterate the project objectives at every meeting

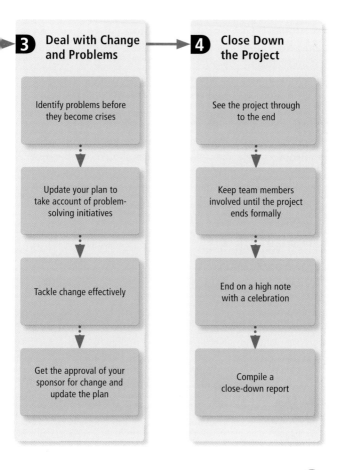

3 Deal with Change and Problems	→	**4** Close Down the Project
Identify problems before they become crises		See the project through to the end
↓		↓
Update your plan to take account of problem-solving initiatives		Keep team members involved until the project ends formally
↓		↓
Tackle change effectively		End on a high note with a celebration
↓		↓
Get the approval of your sponsor for change and update the plan		Compile a close-down report

Integrate Projects

Use the Four Ps of portfolio management and the Four Ps of project implementation to integrate current and future projects into the context of your organization.

Manage a Portfolio of Projects

To ensure that your team works within a culture of projects, you must gain agreement to certain standards.

- **Planning**—Stimulate new projects for operational reasons, such as an improvement in customer service. Look for new projects as a result of a change in strategy, for example a move into a different market. Make sure that all projects link to the overall strategy and goals of the organization.
- **Portfolio**—If you manage a project without paying attention to the other projects around you, you may optimize your use of resources, but at the expense of other projects. This often means that the whole portfolio is not making the best use of all its resources.
- **Projects**—Decide which activities should be managed as projects and which are just business as usual. Make it clear where the discipline of project management is likely to result in improved performance.
- **Process**—Use a common process to define, plan, manage, and control projects across the portfolio to give teams a common language.

Draw a Plan The best way to show how different projects integrate with each other is to draw a plan of the connections between current projects.

Ways to Use Resources Wisely

HIGH IMPACT

- Sharing the key information about projects in terms of their objectives, benefits, and customer focus
- Anticipating the skills and capabilities the project team members will need to carry out the portfolio of projects
- Monitoring the project by referring to key indicators of success

NEGATIVE IMPACT

- Sending out detailed schedules of the many activities that are involved in the project
- Training permanent staff in a skill that only one project will require
- Spending a lot of time and resources monitoring individual action plans

Manage Project Implementation

To ensure the most effective and efficient management of projects, make sure the Four Ps are in place and are being effectively managed:

- **People**—Put in place the right people with the right skills and motivation to implement projects efficiently, and make sure that the organization supports the management of projects.
- **Problems**—Use a process to manage problems as they come up. Success depends on the team's ability to solve problems and adapt plans.
- **Platform**—Make the overall project available on a website. This is a powerful tool for focusing projects on customer expectations and the management and motivation of people.
- **Performance reviews**—Set targets for time, cost, and performance and review them regularly, using your key performance indicators.

TIP Never lose sight of a project's contribution to the organization. It is that contribution that makes the project relevant and successful.

Create a Work/Life Balance

Many of the principles of project management can be applied to putting together a life plan. Leisure time refreshes you and makes you more effective at work, so find the right balance between work and life.

Assess Your Position

Project team members often have two jobs—to achieve their operating targets and play a role in one or more projects. This makes it difficult to maintain a balance between work and play. Without such a balance, work can become stressful and family life impoverished. Work out the balance that suits you. Start from what you are trying to achieve overall and look at three aspects:

- **Objectives**—What are trying to achieve both inside and outside work?
- **Strategy**—How are you going to go about achieving those objectives?
- **Relationships**—Which relationships are important?

Write down your objectives, strategy, and relationships as a starting point. Think about the sort of person you want to be. How do you want to relate to your spouse and children, what sort of a manager do you want to be, how do you want your friends to regard you?

TECHNIQUES *to* practice

In an ideal world, each working day would be a delight. To make that happen you need to practice a positive mental attitude. Recognizing the good things about your life and your job will make you feel more positive about the humdrum.

- Make a list of the positive things in your life.
- Add ten items on the first day, 20 on the second, and so on.
- Read your list every morning and think of more things that you could add to it.
- Consider how many things you have to be grateful for.

Improve the Balance

Decide how much time you want to spend on each aspect of your life—work, family time, hobbies and sports, self-improvement, entertainment. How far is the reality of your life from the ideal you aspire to?

Strike a Balance
Plan to adjust from the current situation to your ideal. The main balance is between life and work. Focus fully when you are at work, but set aside sufficient time for living.

Make Time for What Matters Try not to allow the demands of your job or your career prevent you from spending time with your family and being there for important events.

Use Your Leisure Time If you enjoy sports, make sure you set aside a regular time to participate. Allowing work to prevent you doing so will increase your stress levels.

Index

Picture Credits

The publisher would like to thank the following for their kind permission to reproduce their photographs: Abbreviations key : (l) = left, (c) = center, (r) = right, (t) = top, (b) = below, (cl) = center left, (cr) = center right.

1: Jon Feingersh/zefa/Corbis (l), Altrendo Images/Getty (c), Bruce Ayres/Stone/Getty (r); **2:** Ken Chernus/Taxi/Getty; **3:** Purestock/Alamy (t), Sharon Green/Corbis (c), G. Baden/zefa/Corbis (b); **5:** Sigrid Olsson/The Image Bank/Getty; **7:** Tony Metaxas/Asia Images/Getty; **8:** Jon Feingersh/zefa/Corbis (l), Siri Stafford/Stone+/Getty (cl), Stephen Simpson/Stone/Getty (cr), Dennis O'Clair/Photographer's Choice/Getty (r); **13:** Siri Stafford/Stone+/Getty; **17:** Chris Salvo/Taxi/Getty; **22:** Purestock/Alamy; **33:** Purestock/Alamy; **35:** Altrendo Images/Getty; **41:** Thomas Kruesselmann/zefa/Corbis; **45:** Sie Productions/zefa/Corbis; **49:** Bruce Ayres/Stone/Getty; **57:** Bruce Ayres/Stone/Getty; **61:** Dennis O'Clair/Photographer's Choice/Getty; **62:** Charles Thatcher/Stone/Getty; **68:** Sears Wiebkin/zefa/Corbis; **71:** Helen King/Corbis; **73:** Michael Hemsley; **75:** Johner Images/Getty; **77:** Jon Feingersh/zefa/Corbis; **79:** Luc Porus/Stock Image/Pixland/Alamy; **83:** Michael Shay/Taxi/Getty; **84:** Sigrid Olsson/The Image Bank/Getty; **89:** Sharon Green/Corbis; **93:** Stephen Simpson/Stone/Getty; **97:** Sigrid Olsson/The Image Bank/Getty; **99:** Pete Turner/The Image Bank/Getty; **107:** Pete Cade/Iconica/Getty; **113:** G. Baden/zefa/Corbis; **114:** Jon Feingersh/zefa/Corbis; **117:** Michael Hemsley.

All other images © Dorling Kindersley.

For further information see www.dkimages.com

Authors' acknowledgments

Writing a book for Dorling Kindersley is a most interesting exercise in teamwork. We would like to thank Adèle Hayward and Simon Tuite for their stewardship of the design and the process. Thank you also to the editor, Fiona Biggs, for her constructive feedback and huge contribution to improving the script. Finally, thank you all for making it such an enjoyable task.

Authors' biographies

Andy Bruce is founder and Chief Executive of SofTools—a UK-based business solutions company (www.SofTools.net). Over the last 15 years he has worked with clients in both the public and private sectors to enable senior management visibility and control, and sustained performance improvement. He is also an affiliate lecturer at Henley Management College.

Ken Langdon has a background in sales and marketing in the technology industry. As an independent consultant he has trained salespeople and sales managers in the US, Europe, and Australia, and has advised managers on the coaching and appraisal of their staff. He has also provided strategic guidance for companies including computer giant Hewlett Packard. Ken is the author of a number of books for DK and co-author of several Essential Managers titles, including *Putting Customers First*. He is also one of the authors of DK's *Successful Manager's Handbook*.